BETWEEN the Lamb and THE LION

A new view of Jesus in the book of Revelation—from the cross to His coming

Clifford Goldstein

Pacific Press® Publishing Association
Nampa, Idaho
Oshawa, Ontario, Canada

MW00988446

Edited by B. Russell Holt
Designed by Tim Larson
Cover illustration by Lars Justinen
Typeset in 11/13 New Century Schoolbook

Copyright © 1995 by
Pacific Press® Publishing Association
Printed in the United States of America
All Rights Reserved

Unless otherwise indicated, Scripture quotations are from the
New King James Version.

The author assumes full responsibility for the accuracy of all
facts and quotations cited in this book.

Library of Congress Cataloging-in-Publication Data

Goldstein, Clifford.
    Between the lamb and the lion : a new view of Jesus in
the book of Revelation, from the cross to his coming /
Clifford Goldstein.
        p.   cm.
    Includes bibliographical references.
    ISBN 0-8163-1238-9
    1. Bible. N. T. Revelation—Criticism, interpretation,
etc. 2. Sanctuary doctrine (Seventh-day Adventists)
3. Jesus Christ—Person and offices—Biblical teaching.
4. Seventh-day Adventists—Doctrines. I. Title.
BS2825.2.G625   1995
228'.06—dc20   94-27807
                                                         CIP

99 • 5 4 3 2

Contents

Other Books by Clifford Goldstein

The Saving of America
1844 Made Simple
Best Seller
How Dare You Judge Us, God?
False Balances
A Pause for Peace
Day of the Dragon
The Remnant

To Carnes and Dianne

Chapter
One

BETWEEN THE LAMB
AND THE LION

C ongratulations!
If you're reading this book, it means you survived the giant asteroid predicted to kill one-third of the world's population (a billion or two people) in 1994. This calamity, according to jubilee calculations, was supposed to begin a 1,335-day countdown that ends with the second coming.

Amazingly enough, no killer asteroid wiped out a third of the world in 1994. No doubt, however, just as others have done with failed dates regarding the Sunday law, the shaking, the close of probation, and the second coming, those who blew it predicting the 1994 giant asteroid calamity will find another date close enough to ensure that adherents will continue to send money and yet far enough away so they will continue to send it for a few more years.

"Scoffer," some will say. *"How easy to look back and sneer at failed dates!"* The only trouble with that accusation is that I *wasn't* looking back. Instead, so sure was I that this 1994 calculation was pure malarkey with no root in Scripture, I wrote the above paragraphs (as well as the beginning of this book) *in 1993!*

Of course, date setting, usually based on false interpretations of the books of Daniel and Revelation, isn't just an Adventist headache. In 1857, for example, at the invitation of several members of Congress, Tennessee Methodist minister Fountain Pitts delivered a day-long sermon at the U.S. Capitol on America's prophetic destiny, in which he "proved" that the prophet Daniel had predicted the exact time for the proclamation of the American Declaration of Independence:

> The United States arose at the end of 1,290 symbolic days from the destruction of Jerusalem. . . . Daniel's 70 weeks being equal to 603 years and 1,290 days of solar time, according to the eclipses of the sun. . . . So that if 70 symbolic weeks equaled 600 years and 129 days, 1,290 symbolic days reached from the burning of the temple on the 189th day of the year 68 A.D. to the 4th of July, 1776. . . . Making the starting point at the occasion of the daily sacrifice, which happened, according to astronomy, at sunrise, three minutes past five o'clock a.m. on the day that the temple was burnt, the 1,290 days run out at a quarter to three o'clock p.m., on the 4th day of July, 1776; and, from the best sources of information, the Declaration of Independence was proclaimed at that hour on the glorious Fourth.[1]

Sounds like some of the prophetic literature making the rounds among us.

More recently, Hal Lindsey's inane apocalyptic prognostications in *The Late Great Planet Earth* proclaimed that within forty years of the founding of Israel in 1948, Christ would return. The book sold twenty-eight million copies by 1990 (two years after the deadline!).[2] In his book *There's a New World Coming* (twenty weeks on the *New York Times* bestseller list), Lindsey took the final week of Daniel's seventy-week Messianic prophecy,[3] separated it from the other sixty-nine weeks, placed it somewhere in the future, and applied it to events in Revelation!

"In Chapters 6 through 19 of the Book of Revelation," Lindsey wrote, "we're given an unfolding chronological picture of a future seven-year period of the greatest tribulation this earth will ever experience."[4]

Dates for the secret rapture have been popular too. In the 1980s, former NASA engineer Edgar C. Whisenant wrote a book giving eighty-eight reasons why the rapture would occur in 1988. Taking advantage of the ensuing hoopla, prophecy teacher

Charles Taylor arranged a tour of Israel to coincide with the big day: "We stay at the Intercontinental Hotel right on the Mount of Olives," he advertised, "where you can get the beautiful view of the Eastern Gate and the Temple Mount. And if this is the year of our Lord's return, as we anticipate, you may even ascend to glory from within a few feet of His ascension."[5]

Pat Robertson's prophetic predictions have been as successful as his presidential ambitions. In 1980, convinced that a rare alignment of planets (the now-debunked "Jupiter effect") would coincide with a Russian invasion of Israel, Robertson wrote: "All available economic and military intelligence pinpoints 1982 as the optimum time for such a strike." He said, too, that "Ezekiel indicates enormous earthquake activity and severe hailstones in Israel at the time of the predicted Russian invasion. . . . According to . . . scientists, in 1982 there will be an alignment of planets on the same side of the sun which will exert a sufficiently strong additional gravitational pull on the earth to cause disruptions in the earth's upper atmosphere, radical changes in climactic conditions (hailstones?), and severe earthquakes."[6]

Unfortunately, Adventism hasn't been spared similar silliness, despite inspired testimony against date setting and speculation.[7] No doubt, as the third millennium approaches, our church will be inundated by colorful prophetic charts with multitudinous futuristic reinterpretations of the 1,260 days, the 2,300 days, the 1,335 days, the seventy weeks, and every other time prophecy in Daniel and Revelation. "Time-setting," wrote *Adventist Review* editor William Johnsson, "has plagued Adventists from the beginning. The rash of calculations as the year 2000 draws near isn't anything new, although the number of schemes and excitement seem to be greater than in the past. However, the Seventh-day Adventist Church has never endorsed any of these efforts previously, nor does it give its blessing to any now."[8]

Most prophetic time setting within Adventism (and within Christianity, for that matter) has been based on Daniel and Revelation. As apocalyptic literature, these two books lend themselves to prophetic speculation. Winged leopards, ten-horned beasts, locusts with scorpions' tails, open scrolls, end-time plagues, heavenly judgments, dragons, and beasts rising out of the sea, together with such mysterious numbers as 144,000 and time prophecies about 2,300 evenings and mornings, 1,260 days, seventy weeks, and 1,335 days—all make Daniel and Revelation more exegetically challenging than 1 John or Philemon, for example.

Daniel has been more clearly, and for the most part more accurately, deciphered than Revelation, but only when interpretations have been based on the foundation of the four great world empires: Babylon, Media-Persia, Greece, and Rome. Yet even these powers have been recently subjected to wild and ridiculous reinterpretations—everything from Ayatollah Khomeini to "Satan's one-world government." If prophetic symbols that are as positively identified as are these kingdoms (after all, Scripture actually *names* the first three[9]) have been adulterated, we can imagine what will happen to the more complicated symbols!

"Even a cursory glance at the large number of commentaries on Revelation," writes New Testament scholar Kenneth Strand, "reveals a phenomenally wide array of misunderstandings, misinterpretations, and conclusions that are not only contradictory but frequently also highly speculative."[10]

Despite the difficulties of Revelation, however, one aspect of the book is clear: the centrality of Jesus Christ. The very first verse of the book says it all: "The Revelation of Jesus Christ, which God gave Him to show His servants" (Revelation 1:1). The phrase "the Revelation of Jesus Christ" can be interpreted either as (1) a revelation *from* Jesus or (2) a revelation *about* Him. The immediate context of verse 1 implies the former, because Jesus is "to show His servants" the things that "must shortly take place." The Father revealed the message to Christ, who "sent and signified it by His angel to His servant John" (verse 1). Red-letter editions of the Bible show that Christ Himself is speaking throughout the book. No doubt, Revelation is *from* Jesus.

But it is a revelation *about* Him as well, and to miss that aspect is to miss the crucial element. Interpreters often focus on the beasts, the harlot, the numbers, and the dragon, but not on the Lamb, the main figure of the Apocalypse. Martin Luther, for example, wrote: "My spirit cannot accommodate itself to this book [Revelation]. There is one sufficient reason for the small esteem in which I hold it—that Christ is neither taught in it or recognized."[11]

Christ neither taught or recognized? The first verse of the book begins with Jesus, the last verse ends with Him, and He appears all throughout. He is called Jesus or Christ (Revelation 1:1, 2, 5, 9; 11:15; 14:12; 19:10; 20:4, 6; 22:16, 20, 21); the faithful witness (1:5); the firstborn from the dead (1:5); the Son of Man (1:13; 14:14); He who lives (1:18); He who searches the minds and hearts (2:23); the Lion of the tribe of Judah (5:5); the Lamb (5:6, 8, 12, 13; 6:1; 7:9, 10, 14, 17; 12:11; 13:8; 14:1, 4, 10; 15:3; 17:14; 19:7, 9; 21:9, 14, 22, 23, 27; 22:1, 3); Faithful and True (19:11); the Word of God (19:13); King of kings and Lord of lords (19:16); the Alpha and Omega (21:6); and the Bright and Morning Star (22:16). Under one symbol or another, Christ and His saving activities are woven throughout Revelation. He—not beasts, dates, or numbers—is the thread, the motif, the central figure who unifies the Apocalypse.

Thus, any systematic attempt to understand Revelation must center on Jesus, the One upon whom the book centers. Though numerous speculations exist about the identity of the beast with ten horns, the 1,260 days, the harlot with a golden cup in her hand, and the locusts with crowns of gold and women's hair— the identity of Christ is certain, and He is more significant than the harlot, the dragon, or the numbers.

So much is known about Christ because the rest of the Bible focuses on Him as well. The first sixty-five books tell enough about Jesus to help us decipher His role in the sixty-sixth. It's the understanding of Christ and His role in earlier books that unveils Him and His role in the last.[12] "The visions of Revelation," wrote Graeme Goldsworthy, "must be read in the light of the unified message of the whole Bible, which reaches its goal in Jesus Christ."[13] Like a complex math problem, the known elements must be dealt with before we tackle the more difficult aspects. And because Christ is the known element in Revelation, all attempts at interpretation must begin with Him.

Before one begins deciphering Christ's role in the Apocalypse, however, a few more facts need explaining. First, most contemporary scholars, along with the early church fathers, have dated the writing of Revelation to the reign of the Roman emperor Domitian, A.D. 81-96, which would make it the last canonical book. "The testimony of early Christian writers is almost unanimous that the book of Revelation was written during the reign of Domitian."[14]

Second, this date, or even a suggested earlier one under the persecution of Nero (A.D. 64), means that the book was written long after the death and resurrection of Christ, which happened in A.D. 31.[15]

Third, in the first verse of Revelation, John wrote: "The Revelation of Jesus Christ, which God gave Him to show His servants—things which *must shortly take place*" (Revelation 1:1). Thus, whether under Nero or Domitian, Revelation was written years after Christ's earthly ministry. His cry, "It is finished" (John 19:30), echoed decades before John wrote the book.

Thus, if John was writing about things that "must shortly take place," then he was dealing with events not only after his own time but long after the death and resurrection of Christ. And if so much of Revelation is about Jesus and what He is doing, then the book must be about the activity of Christ *after the cross*.

As the ensuing chapters will show, Calvary is depicted in Revelation. In fact, Christ's death forms the foundation of the book. Everything that Jesus has done for us comes from Calvary, so how could the Apocalypse be about Jesus and not be about the cross? "It pleased the Father that in Him all the fullness should dwell, and by Him to reconcile all things to Himself, by Him, whether things on earth or things in heaven, having made peace through the blood of His cross" (Colossians 1:19, 20).

The point is that both the Old and New Testaments teach that Christ's work for humankind didn't end with His death. Christ certainly completed the work He came to do while on earth as the "Lamb of God who takes away the sin of the world" (John 1:29). On the eve of His death, He prayed: "I have glorified You on the earth. I have finished the work which You have given Me to do" (John 17:4). But Jesus' earthly work—even as our perfect substitute—wasn't His only work. His death—the ransom for every soul (see Matthew 20:28; Mark 10:45; 1 Timothy 2:6)—as complete as it was in itself, didn't mark the final phase of the plan of salvation. Jesus began doing something new after His death and resurrection.[16]

Which was . . . ?

"But Christ came as High Priest of the good things to come, with the greater and more perfect tabernacle not made with hands, that is, not of this creation" (Hebrews 9:11).

"Seeing then that we have a great High Priest who has passed through the heavens, Jesus the Son of God, let us hold fast our confession" (Hebrews 4:14).

"Having been perfected, He became the author of eternal salvation to all who obey Him, called by God as High Priest 'according to the order of Melchizedek' " (Hebrews 5:9, 10.)

"He, because He continues forever, has an unchangeable priesthood. Therefore He is also able to save to the uttermost those who come to God through Him, since He ever lives to make intercession for them. For such a High Priest was fitting for us, who is holy, harmless, undefiled, separate from sinners, and has become higher than the heavens" (Hebrews 7:24-26).

"Now this is the main point of the things we are saying: We have such a High Priest, who is seated at the right hand of the throne of the Majesty in the heavens, a Minister of the sanctuary and of the true tabernacle which the Lord erected, and not man" (Hebrews 8:1, 2).

The New Testament book of Hebrews points believers to Christ's ministry in the heavenly sanctuary. While the Gospels focus upon Christ's work on earth, the book of Hebrews—building upon that work—directs readers to Christ's work in heaven as our great High Priest.[17]

"Jesus Christ," writes Edward Heppenstall, "offered Himself to God to be a sacrifice for sin on the cross. Following His ascension He ministers at the right hand of the Father in the heavenly sanctuary as High Priest and Mediator between God and man."[18]

BETWEEN THE LAMB AND THE LION

If, therefore, Revelation deals not only with the cross but also with Christ *after* the cross, and if Hebrews shows Christ, after the cross, as our High Priest—then Revelation must also be about Christ as High Priest!

Many Christians miss this crucial point. "The Apocalypse of John," writes Jean-Pierre Prevost, "is uniquely devoted to the decisive event of the life of Jesus, His death, and resurrection."[19]

But what about Christ as the High Priest in the heavenly sanctuary? Christ's life, death, and resurrection didn't end His work; on the contrary, they laid the foundation for His heavenly priesthood—the focus, not only of Hebrews, but of Revelation. Most Christians who study Christology in Revelation deal with Christ as the Lamb at His first coming, the Lion at His second, or both, but they miss His crucial role in between.

"It is this relationship of the first and second comings which provides the structure of John's thought in the book of Revelation," writes Graeme Goldsworthy. "It is the relationship of the suffering Christ to the Christ who is manifested in glory. It is the relationship of the Lamb to the Lion."[20]

But what about the 1,900 years (so far) between the Lamb and the Lion, when Jesus has been High Priest in the heavenly sanctuary?

This is the theme of *Between the Lamb and the Lion*: Christ the High Priest in the heavenly sanctuary as depicted in Revelation. Revelation teaches not only that Christ ministers in the heavenly sanctuary, it also teaches the concept of a two-phased, or two-apartment, ministry, long a fundamental and unique teaching of Adventism.[21] This book will show that the two-apartment concept, founded upon Christ's work on the cross, forms the basis of the Apocalypse and is crucial to its understanding. *Between the Lamb and the Lion* shows that the second phase of Christ's heavenly ministry is the work of judgment, which has its counterpart in the yearly Day of Atonement ceremony of the earthly sanctuary service, and how this judgment is inseparably linked to Calvary. Though the focus is upon Jesus' work in the sanctuary, *Between the Lamb and the Lion* reveals how that work must always be viewed through the cross.

14

No Adventist belief has faced more attack—both from within and without the church—than the two-phase work of Christ in the heavenly sanctuary, especially the concept of the pre-advent judgment associated with the second phase.[22] Therefore, it's crucial that Adventists understand not only the scriptural basis for this belief, but its importance and its cross-centeredness as well.[23]

In this book, then, I have two main goals: to confirm the scriptural basis of these teachings and to show that Christ's ministry in the heavenly sanctuary—far from being in tension with the cross—is the means by which Christ applies it to our lives.

And that is what I will do. Unless, of course, the giant asteroid stops me. . . .

1. Fountain Pitts, "Defense of Armageddon," *National Intelligence*, (Feb. 24, 1857), 10, v-vii. Quoted in Paul Boyer, *When Time Shall Be No More* (Cambridge, Mass.: Harvard University Press, 1992), 85.

2. Hal Lindsey, *The Late Great Planet Earth* (Grand Rapids, Mich.: Zondervan, 1980), 43.

3. See Daniel 9:24-27.

4. Hal Lindsey, *There's a New World Coming* (New York: Bantam, 1973), 83.

5. *Bible Prophecy News* 17:7 (1988), 11. Quoted in William Alnor, *Soothsayers of the Second Advent* (Old Tappan, N. J.: Fleming H. Revell, 1989), 29.

6. Pat Robertson, *Pat Robertson's Perspective* (February/March 1980), 3.

7. See *Evangelism* 221; *Early Writings* 22, 75; *Testimonies for the Church*, 1:72, 73, 307; 4:308; 6:440; *Selected Messages*, 1:188, 189; 2: 73, 113, 114; *Testimonies to Ministers,* 54, 55, 60, 61; *Spiritual Gifts*, 2:122, 123.

8. William Johnsson, "Will Jesus Come in 1994? Part 3," *Adventist Review* (April 29, 1993), 4.

9. Babylon (see Daniel 2:38), Media-Persia (see Daniel 8:20), and Greece (see Daniel 8:21) are all specifically mentioned by name. Only the fourth kingdom, Rome (both stages) isn't. For a possible explanation why Rome wasn't named, see "Whatever Happened to Rome?" *Liberty Alert* (August-September 1993), 1.

10. Kenneth Strand, "Foundation Principles of Interpretation," in *Symposium on Revelation,* vol. 1, Frank Holbrook, ed. (Silver Spring,

Md.: General Conference of Seventh-day Adventists, 1992), 4.

11. Quoted in G. B. Caird, *The Revelation of St. John the Divine* (New York: Harper and Row, 1966), 2.

12. "In the Revelation, all the books of the Bible meet and end" (*The Acts of the Apostles*, 585).

13. Graeme Goldsworthy, *The Lion and the Lamb: The Gospel in Revelation* (New York: Thomas Nelson, 1984), 17.

14. *SDA Bible Commentary*, 7:721.

15. "After studying the relevant chronological materials in some detail, I would estimate that the year of Jesus' crucifixion probably could be narrowed down to either A.D. 30 or 31; other earlier or later dates seem considerably less likely" (William Shea, "The Prophecy of Daniel 9:24-27," in *70 Weeks, Leviticus, Nature of Prophecy,* Frank Holbrook, ed. [Washington, D.C.: Biblical Research Institute, 1986], 103).

16. See Clifford Goldstein, *False Balances* (Boise, Idaho: Pacific Press Publishing Association, 1992).

17. "The intercession of Christ in man's behalf in the sanctuary above is as essential to the plan of salvation as was His death on the cross. By His death He began the work which after His resurrection He ascended to complete in Heaven" (*The Great Controversy*, 489).

18. Edward Heppenstall, *Our High Priest* (Washington, D.C.: Review and Herald, 1972), 49.

19. Jean Pierre Prevost, *How to Read the Apocalypse* (New York: Crossroad, 1993), 8.

20. Goldsworthy, 28.

21. "There is a sanctuary in heaven, the true tabernacle which the Lord set up and not man. In it Christ ministers in our behalf, making available to believers the benefits of His atoning sacrifice offered once for all on the cross. He was inaugurated as our Great High Priest and began His intercessory ministry at the time of His ascension. In 1844, at the end of the prophetic 2300 days, He entered the second and last phase of His atoning ministry. It is a work of investigative judgment which is part of the ultimate disposition of sin" (*Seventh-day Adventists Believe* [Washington, D.C.: General Conference of Seventh-day Adventists, 1988], 312).

22. For a survey of criticism of the teaching, see Arnold V. Wallenkampf, "Challengers to the Doctrine of the Sanctuary," in *Doctrine of the Sanctuary*, Frank Holbrook, ed. (Silver Spring, Md.: General Conference of Seventh-day Adventists, 1989), 197-216.

23. "The subject of the sanctuary and the investigative judgment

should be clearly understood by the people of God. All need a knowledge for themselves of the position and work of their great High Priest. Otherwise it will be impossible for them to exercise the faith which is essential at this time, or to occupy the position which God designs them to fill. . . . The sanctuary in heaven is the very center of Christ's work in behalf of men. It concerns every soul living upon the earth. It opens to view the plan of redemption, bringing us down to the very close of time, and revealing the triumphant issue of the contest between righteousness and sin. It is of utmost importance that all should thoroughly investigate these subjects, and be able to give an answer to everyone that asketh them a reason of the hope that is in them" *(The Great Controversy*, 488, 489).

"As a people, we should be earnest students of prophecy; we should not rest until we become intelligent in regard to the subject of the sanctuary, which is brought out in the visions of Daniel and John" *(Evangelism*, 222, 223).

Chapter
Two

THE FAITHFUL WITNESS

During the Second World War, Eric Erickson became a "counterfeit traitor." Because of his extensive ties to the German oil industry, the Swedish businessman had been recruited by the Allies to spy on Hitler's war machine. No one in Sweden knew, except Erickson's wife; everyone had to believe that he was a Nazi. His life depended on it.

Once, in a Stockholm restaurant, a Jewish friend approached Erickson at his table. The counterfeit traitor immediately berated him before other patrons. "I have warned you repeatedly to stop bothering me with your disgusting Jewish business propositions!" he raged. "I do not do business with Jews. So take yourself out of here at once."

The next day Erickson received a note from his friend saying he couldn't believe that Erickson really felt that way about him, that his attitude must have a "special purpose," and that "if I can ever help, let me know." Erickson immediately destroyed the paper and continued spying.[1]

Apparently, his Jewish friend knew enough about Erickson, his character, his motives, and his heart, that despite the scene in the restaurant, he trusted Erickson anyway.

Is not such a trust similar to what the Lord wants from us? Has not our heavenly Father been revealing enough about His character, His motives, and His heart so that His people should love and trust Him no matter the circumstances? Has not the Lord been crying out for human beings' love for thousands of years?

Of course. That's why the first and greatest commandment is to "love the Lord your God with all your heart, with all your soul, and with all your mind" (Matthew 22:37).[2] Yet how can we love the Lord unless we know Him? We can't, and so Jesus Christ came in the flesh to reveal the Father so that we could better know and therefore love Him.[3] "He who has seen Me," Jesus said, "has seen the Father" (John 14:9).[4]

It is through Jesus, then, who was God's words, God's thoughts, God's character encapsulated in flesh, bone, and blood, that God has made Himself known to us.[5] It is through Jesus, the "express image" of His Father's person (Hebrews 1:3), that we can know God the way we need to know Him in order to love Him the way we need to love Him, even the way we are commanded to love Him. And it is through Jesus, our perfect substitute and surety, that we have eternal life. "And this is eternal life, that they may *know* You, the only true God, and Jesus Christ whom You have sent" (John 17:3, emphasis supplied).

Yet Jesus hasn't been on earth for almost two thousand years. We can't look into His eyes as Mary did. We can't put our fingers in His scars as Thomas did. We can't lay our heads across His bosom as John did. So, instead, the Father has sent the Holy Spirit to guide us "into all truth" (John 16:13). And through the work of the Spirit in our lives, Jesus can be revealed to us through nature, prayer, providences, and the Bible.[6]

Of all these ways, the Bible has provided the most forceful, clear, and unmistakable revelation of Christ. And the book of Revelation offers a unique contribution to that manifestation.

In it John "bore witness to the word of God, and to the testimony of Jesus Christ, and to all things that he saw" (Revelation 1:2). Both the verb *bore witness* and the noun *testimony* come from the same root that later formed the English word *martyr.* In Greek, the root can mean "a witness" (as a noun) or "to testify" (as a verb). Thus, besides the "Revelation of Jesus Christ" (Revelation 1:1), John also gives witness to or testifies to the "word of God" and "the testimony of Jesus Christ."

When John says that in the book of Revelation he is bearing witness to "the word of God," most commentators interpret that word of God not as Jesus, the Word of God, who became flesh (see John 1:1, 14).[7] Instead, most view it as the message of God, as in the phrase, "Hear ye the word of the Lord, O King."[8] Thus, the "word of God" is a specific message from God and, in Revelation, that specific message is the gospel of Jesus Christ.

John, for example, said that he was exiled to Patmos because of the "word of God" (Revelation 1:9), that is, the gospel he preached. Under the fifth seal, John viewed the martyrs slain "for the word of God" (Revelation 6:9), the gospel message they proclaimed. John wrote, too, about the souls of those beheaded for "the word of God" (Revelation 20:4), again, the gospel, which brought them the world's condemnation.

The "testimony of Jesus," also known as the "spirit of prophecy" (Revelation 19:10), is the prophetic gift manifested to John by Jesus—the gift that, ultimately, reveals the gospel.[9]

Thus, the first two verses of the Apocalypse show that the book is a revelation of the good news given by Christ Himself. No wonder, then, that the first description of Christ in Revelation points to the gospel. "And from Jesus Christ, the faithful witness, the firstborn from the dead, and the ruler over the kings of the earth. To Him who loved us and washed us from our sins in His own blood" (Revelation 1:5).

This verse overflows with references to Christ's life, death, and resurrection. He is "the faithful witness," a reference to His earthly sojourn, in which He faithfully, even perfectly, exemplified the truth about the character of God. "For this cause I was born," He said, "and for this cause I have come into the world, that I should bear witness to the truth" (John 18:37). Jesus is, writes Philip Edgcumbe Hughes, "altogether trustworthy, who throughout his earthly mission set us an example by unfailingly maintaining a faithful witness in the face of antagonism, suffering, and death."[10] Jesus was the "faithful witness," too, as He wrought out the perfect righteousness that made Him our Saviour. "Though He was a Son, yet He learned obedience by the things which He suffered. And having been perfected, He became the author of eternal salvation to all who obey Him" (Hebrews 5:8, 9).

The description "the firstborn from the dead" (Revelation 1:5) deals with His resurrection. "By his resurrection," writes G. R.

Beasley-Murray, "he has become the first born of the dead and brought life to the children of God."[11] Though Jesus wasn't the first person ever to rise from the dead, "He may be regarded," according to the *SDA Bible Commentary*, "as the first in the sense that all others resurrected before and after Him gained their freedom from the bonds of death only by virtue of His triumph over the grave."[12] This concept has been linked, also, to the wave-sheaf and firstfruits offering of the Hebrew feasts. "Now Christ is risen from the dead, and has become the firstfruits of those who have fallen asleep" (1 Corinthians 15:20).[13]

And, of course, the phrase He "washed us from our sins in His own blood" (Revelation 1:5; other alternatives read "loosed us" or "freed us") points to Christ's death on the cross, the foundation of the plan of salvation. By His death Christ paid the complete penalty for sin, so that all of us can be reconciled to God through the blood of Christ. "But now in Christ Jesus you who once were far off have been made near by the blood of Christ" (Ephesians 2:13). Through His blood, Jesus has freed us from the penalty of our sins. "In Him we have redemption through His blood, the forgiveness of sins, according to the riches of His grace" (Ephesians 1:7). And not only are we justified, forgiven, and redeemed by His blood, but we are cleansed as well. "If we walk in the light as He is in the light, we have fellowship with one another, and the blood of Jesus Christ His Son cleanses us from all sin" (1 John 1:7).

Thus, before Revelation explodes into visions of beasts, locusts, and wars, it begins with Jesus' life, death, and resurrection. Before it delves into His heavenly ministry, it delves into His earthly ministry, because only after His earthly work could Jesus do His heavenly work.

Verily he took not on him the nature of angels; but he took on him the seed of Abraham. Wherefore in all things it behooved him to be made like unto his brethren, that he might be a merciful and faithful high priest in things pertaining to God, to make reconciliation for the sins of the people. For in that he himself hath suffered being tempted, he is able to succor them that are tempted (Hebrews 2:16-18, KJV).

By stressing Christ's earthly mission, Revelation 1:5 lays the foundation for what He does in the rest of the book, which culminates in His second coming and, ultimately, in a new heaven and earth (Revelation 21:1).

The phrase "washed us from our sins in his own blood" (Revelation 1:5) also introduces a new element—the sanctuary—early on in the Apocalypse. Divorced from the background of the sanctuary, being washed in blood makes no more sense than does being warmed by ice. Blood doesn't cleanse, it stains—except in the Israelite sanctuary service, where blood did, indeed, cleanse. For example, on the Day of Atonement, after a bullock and a goat were slain, the High Priest took "some of the blood of the bull and some of the blood of the goat, and put it on the horns of the altar all around. Then he shall sprinkle some of the blood on it with his finger seven times, *cleanse* it, and sanctify it from the uncleanness of the children of Israel" (Leviticus 16:18, 19, emphasis supplied).[14]

When John the Baptist looked up and saw Jesus, he didn't cry out, "Behold! The Porcupine of God who takes away the sin of the world." Why? Because it would have made no sense. Nothing about a porcupine would give it particular meaning to anyone who heard John's words. When he cried out, however, " 'Behold! The *Lamb* of God who takes away the sin of the world' " (John 1:29, emphasis supplied), the imagery immediately evoked the temple service, the only context that makes John's words comprehensible.

In the story of Abraham and Isaac on Mount Moriah, Abraham said to his son, "God will provide for Himself the lamb for a burnt offering" (Genesis 22:8), a phrase understood by Christians as a prophetic oracle of Christ's death.[15] Though in Abraham's day the sanctuary service itself had not yet been initiated, it was foreshadowed in the sacrificial system of the patriarchs—itself a type, or symbol, of Christ's sacrifice.

In Isaiah 53, the prophet writes that the Lord will make His Suffering Servant (Jesus) "an offering for sin" (verse 10). That phrase is encapsulated in a Hebrew word meaning "to offend" or "to be guilty." In its noun form, as it appears in Isaiah 53:10, it has been translated as "trespassing offering" or "guilt offering," both of which were parts of the Israelite sanctuary service.

In the Messianic prophecy of Daniel 9:24-27, Gabriel said that Christ's death would "bring an end to sacrifice and offering" (verse 27).[16] Once Jesus died, writes William Shea, "meaning had gone out of those sacrifices because Christ the great Antitype fulfilled their ultimate significance with His death on the cross (Matthew 27:50-51; Luke 23:45-46)."[17] The point, again, is that Christ's death is described in the context of the Hebrew sanctuary service.

For this reason, then, the New Testament writers developed their theology of Christ's life and death from the sanctuary types and symbols.[18] When Peter wrote that believers are not redeemed through corruptible things but through "the precious blood of Christ, as of a lamb without blemish and without spot" (1 Peter 1:19), the imagery came from the Old Testament sanctuary service, in which the sacrificial animals had to be without physical defects.[19]

At the moment Jesus died, the Passover lamb, about to be slaughtered, escaped, and the veil between the Holy and the Most Holy Place in the earthly sanctuary was torn apart. Both the escape of the lamb and the rending of the veil show how closely Christ's death was linked to the sanctuary service.[20] No wonder Paul wrote that "Christ, our Passover, was sacrificed for us" (1 Corinthians 5:7).

The concept of Christ's atoning blood derives its meaning only from the sanctuary service. "For the life of the flesh is in the blood, and I have given it to you upon the altar to make atonement for your souls; *for it is the blood that makes atonement for the soul*" (Leviticus 17:11, emphasis supplied). The blood of Christ is repeatedly described in the New Testament as the vital element of salvation. Thus the expressions "purchased with His own blood" (Acts 20:28), "redemption through His blood" (Ephesians 1:7), "peace through the blood" (Colossians 1:20), "sanctify the people with His own blood" (Hebrews 13:12), "sprinkling of the blood" (1 Peter 1:2), "having now been justified by His blood" (Romans 5:9) must be understood from the sanctuary service.

The book of Hebrews, perhaps more than any other book in the New Testament, shows how inseparable the cross is from the sanctuary. The Levitical sanctuary forms the context upon which the book is based. "Even a casual reading of Hebrews," writes Dr. Alberto R. Treiyer, "indicates that its apostolic author is comparing and contrasting the Levitical system (first covenant; earthly sanctuary; animal sacrifices; human priesthood) with a new system of worship inaugurated by Christ (new covenant; heavenly sanctuary; Christ's own atoning death and priesthood)."[21]

For instance, Hebrews deals with issues of purification and cleansing of sin, often in the context of blood, which again makes sense only in the sanctuary context. "The theological argument of Hebrews," writes William Johnsson, "centers in the cultus (the sanctuary service). And the cultus—as set forth in Hebrews—revolves around the problem of defilement and purification."[22]

When Hebrews refers to Jesus as the "High Priest,"[23] it automatically evokes the Hebrew sanctuary. The statement that "not with the blood of goats and calves, but with His own blood He entered the Most Holy Place once for all, having obtained eternal redemption" (Hebrews 9:12) can be understood only in relation to the sanctuary. When Hebrews 7:27 says that Jesus "does not need daily, as those high priests, to offer up sacrifices, first for His own sins and then for the people's, for this He did once for all when He offered up Himself," the Bible irrefutably links Christ's sacrifice to the Levitical sanctuary ritual.

The point is simple: The cross and what Jesus accomplished for us there cannot be separated from the sanctuary service. The symbolism surrounding the cross derives its meaning only from the sanctuary. Substitution, blood atonement, cleansing, justification, sanctification, and redemption—the central elements of what the cross accomplished—are inseparably linked to the Jewish economy. To separate the cross from that is to separate it from the one setting that makes it meaningful.

Thus, when Revelation refers to "the Lamb" (6:16) or the "Lamb who was slain" (5:12) or "the blood of the Lamb" (7:14), all references to the cross—these are all sanctuary images. A lamb in and of itself means nothing, much less one that was slain and bloody. The imagery, like the cross itself, becomes significant only through the sanctuary.

Also, despite its strong emphasis regarding Christ's first coming and the sanctuary implications that this first coming automatically evokes, Revelation, early on, tells about His second coming as well. In two verses, following the sweeping imagery regarding the first advent, Revelation graphically describes the second advent. "Behold, He is coming with clouds, and every eye will see Him, and they also who pierced Him. And all the tribes of the earth will mourn because of Him. Even so, Amen" (1:7).

The two events—His first and second comings—are probably so closely linked because Jesus can do what He does at His second coming only by virtue of what He accomplished at His first coming. The whole purpose of the first coming was to prepare the way for the second. The first, without the hope and promise of the second, means nothing. What would Christ's earthly life and death have accomplished for humanity if they ultimately didn't culminate in His returning to earth to retrieve His redeemed people and take them with Him to heaven? The second coming is the culmination of the first.

"The first coming of Christ, the gospel-event, establishes the significance of the second coming of Christ. Perhaps one of the greatest reasons for misunderstanding the book of Revelation is the failure to grasp the relationship of the first and second comings of Christ."[24]

Though the end of Revelation storms with graphic illustrations of the second coming, John doesn't wait until the end of the book to tell about it. Even before his first vision, John describes the second coming. Why?

John lived in an era of anti-Christian sentiment. He knew that the church was to face difficult times. Though written to comfort and teach the church in all ages, Revelation was especially important for the church of the first century as it was about to suffer incredible persecution.[25] Perhaps, because of this threat, John wrote about the second coming first, to give the church hope before his description of the martyrs and those who would be beheaded, exiled, and persecuted for "the word of God."

"The object of the Apocalypse," writes R. H. Charles, "was to encourage the faithful to resist even to death the blasphemous claims of the State, and to proclaim the coming victory of the cause of God and of His Christ."[26] John wanted to encourage the church with the promise that despite their sufferings, in the end, Christ will return and truth will reign triumphant, and he didn't want to wait until the end of the book to do it.

Thus, within the first seven verses of Revelation, Christ's first and second comings are depicted. He is, indeed, the Lamb who was slain and the Lion of the tribe of Judah who will return in glory.

But what about His role in between?

---

1. Alexander Kline, *The Counterfeit Traitor* (New York: Henry Holt and Company, 1958), 20.

2. See Deuteronomy 6:6; 11:1, 3; 13:3; 19:9; 30:6, 16, 20; Joshua 22:5.

3. "All that man needs to know or can know of God has been revealed in the life and character of His Son. . . . Taking humanity upon Him, Christ came to be one with humanity and at the same time to reveal our heavenly Father to sinful human beings" *(Testimonies for the Church*, 8:286).

"By coming to dwell with us, Jesus was to reveal God both to men and to angels. He was the Word of God,—God's thought made audible" *(The Desire of Ages*, 19).

4. "Therefore the Lord Himself will give you a sign: Behold, the virgin shall conceive, and bear a Son, and shall call his name Immanuel" (Isaiah 7:14). Immanuel means "God with us."

"In the beginning was the Word, and the Word was with God, and the Word was God. . . . And the Word became flesh and dwelt among us" (John 1:1, 14).

5. "Let this mind be in you which was also in Christ Jesus, who, being in the form of God, did not consider it robbery to be equal with God, but made Himself of no reputation, taking the form of a servant, and coming in the likeness of men. And being found in appearance as a man, He humbled Himself and became obedient to the point of death,

even the death of the cross" (Philippians 2:5-8).

6. "God has bound our hearts to Him by unnumbered tokens in heaven and in earth. Through the things of nature, and the deepest and tenderest earthly ties that human hearts can know, He has sought to reveal Himself to us. Yet these but imperfectly represent His love" (*Steps to Christ*, 10).

7. One prominent exception is J. Massyngberde Ford, who translates it "the Word of God" and wrote that "John bears witness to the *Logos*" (J. Massyngberde Ford, *Revelation*, The Anchor Bible [New York: Doubleday, 1975], 373, 374).

8. Jeremiah 22:2. The phrase "the word of the Lord" is used dozens upon dozens of times, possibly hundreds, in the Old Testament, particularly among the messages of Jeremiah and Ezekiel.

9. "John here refers back to 'the Revelation of Jesus Christ, which God gave unto him' (v.1). 'The word of God,' 'the testimony of Jesus,' and 'all things that he saw' all refer to the same thing—'the Revelation' of v. 1'" (*SDA Bible Commentary*, 7:730. See also Gerhard Pfandl, "The Remnant Church and the Spirit of Prophecy," in *Symposium on Revelation*, vol. 2, Frank Holbrook, ed. [Silver Spring, Md.: General Conference of Seventh-day Adventists, 1992], 295-334.

10. Philip Edgcumbe Hughes, *The Book of Revelation* (Grand Rapids, Mich.: William B. Eerdmans, 1990), 18.

11. G. R. Beasley-Murray, *Revelation* (Grand Rapids, Mich.: William B. Eerdmans, 1983), 56.

12. *SDA Bible Commentary*, 7:732.

13. "The word 'firstborn' may be a reference to the simple fact that Jesus was the first to rise from the dead, and as such is the first fruits of the resurrection (1 Cor. 15:20)" (George Eldon Ladd, *A Commentary on Revelation* [Grand Rapids, Mich.: William B. Eerdmans, 1972], 25).

"Christ was the first fruits of them that slept. This very scene, the resurrection of Christ from the dead, was observed in type by the Jews at one of their sacred feasts. . . . They came up to the Temple when the first fruits had been gathered in, and held a feast of thanksgiving. The first fruits of the harvest crop were sacredly dedicated to the Lord. That crop was not to be appropriated for the benefit of man. The first ripe fruit was dedicated as a thank offering to God. He was acknowledged as the Lord of the harvest. When the first heads of grain ripened in the field, they were carefully gathered, and when the people went up to Jerusalem, they were presented to the Lord, waving the ripened sheaf before Him as a thank offering. After this ceremony the sickle could be put to the wheat, and it could be gathered into sheaves" (*Manuscript* 115, 1897).

14. For more, see Angel Rodriguez, "Transfer of Sin in Leviticus;" Alberto R. Treiyer, "The Day of Atonement As Related to the Contamination and Purification of the Sanctuary," in *70 Weeks, Leviticus, Nature of Prophecy*, Frank Holbrook, ed. (Washington, D.C.: Biblical Research Institute, 1986), 169-197; 198-258.

15. "It was to impress Abraham's mind with the reality of the gospel, as well as to test his faith, that God commanded him to slay his son. The agony which he endured during the dark days of that fearful trial was permitted that he might understand from his own experience something of the greatness of the sacrifice made by the infinite God for man's redemption. No other test could have caused Abraham such torture of the soul as did the suffering of his son. God gave his Son to a death of agony and shame. The angels who witnessed the humiliation and soul anguish of the Son of God were not permitted to interpose, as in the case of Isaac. There was no voice to cry, 'It is enough.' To save the fallen race, the King of Glory yielded up His life. What stronger proof can be given of the infinite compassion and love of God?" (*Patriarchs and Prophets*, 154).

16. "The Hebrew word for sacrifice, *zebah*, refers to animal sacrifices in general. The Hebrew word for offerings, *minhah*, is used commonly in Exodus to refer to cereal offerings. Here it probably refers to nonanimal sacrifices as a class. Together these two words encompass all animal and nonanimal sacrifices—the sacrificial system as a whole" (William Shea, "The Prophecy of Daniel 9:24-27," in *70 Weeks, Leviticus, Nature of Prophecy*. Frank Holbrook, ed. [Washington, D.C.: Biblical Research Institute of the General Conference of Seventh-day Adventists, 1986], 96).

17. Ibid.

18. See Angel Rodriguez, "Salvation by Sacrificial Substitution," *Journal of the Adventist Theological Society* (1992), 49-77.

19. See Leviticus 1:3, 10; 3:1; 4:3, 22, 28; 5:15, 18; 6:6; 9:2; 14:10; Ezekiel 43:22, 23, 25 are just some of the examples.

20. Matthew 27:51; Mark 15:38; Luke 23:45. See also *The Desire of Ages*, 756, 757.

21. Alberto R. Treiyer, "Antithetical or Correspondence Typology," in *Issues in the Book of Hebrews*, Frank Holbrook, ed. (Silver Spring, Md.: Biblical Research Institute, 1989), 187.

A casual glance at non-Adventist literature on Hebrews shows how it also links the book to the ancient Hebrew system.

THE FAITHFUL WITNESS

"Having established the superiority of the high priesthood of Christ, our author now proceeds to relate His high priesthood to the themes of covenant, sanctuary, and sacrifice, with which the Aaronic priesthood was closely bound up" (F. F. Bruce, *The Epistle to the Hebrews* [Grand Rapids, Mich.: William B. Eerdmans, 1964], 163).

"There is first the question whether Hebrews presupposed that the temple service is operative or not. Why are the references to sacrifice always biblical, quoting or alluding to Exodus and Leviticus, speaking of tent and never referring to the existing temple?" (Barnabas Lindars, *The Theology of the Letter to the Hebrews* [New York: Cambridge University Press, 1991], 19).

"The importance of the priesthood, the temple, and the treasury of merits to the Jewish doctrine of atonement provides the basis for the author's Christology and understanding of the role of Jesus. Jews and Christians of New Testament times thought of heaven in terms of temple surroundings" (George Wesley Buchanan, *To the Hebrews*, Anchor Bible Series, vol. 36 [Garden City, N.Y.: Doubleday & Company, 1972], 83).

22. William Johnsson, "Defilement/Purification in Hebrews," ibid., 82.

23. Hebrews 3:1; 4:14, 15; 5:10; 6:20; 7:26; 9:11.

24. Goldsworthy, 28.

25. "It was at this critical time in the history of the church that John was sentenced to banishment. Never had his voice been needed by the church as now. Nearly all his former associates in the ministry had suffered martyrdom. The remnant of believers was facing fierce opposition. To all outward appearance the day was not far distant when the enemies of the church of Christ would triumph" *(The Acts of the Apostles*, 581).

26. R. H. Charles, *Revelation: The International Critical Commentary* (Edinburgh: T & T Clark, 1985), xxii.

Chapter
Three
THE SON OF MAN

Though primarily a book of visions, Revelation begins with John telling who he is, where he is, why he is there, what is happening to him, and what he is doing. Not until chapter 1, verse 12 does he record a vision:

> Then I turned to see the voice that spoke with me. And having turned I saw seven golden lampstands, and in the midst of the seven lampstands One like the Son of Man, clothed with a garment down to the feet and girded about the chest with a golden band. His head and His hair were white like wool, as white as snow, and His eyes like a flame of fire (verses 12-14).

The first thing John records as seeing in vision, then, is "seven golden lampstands," or candlesticks. This image relates directly to the sanctuary, specifically to the seven-branched candlestick (the menorah)[1] found in the first apartment of both the wilderness tabernacle and the temple in Jerusalem.[2] Much has been written about the menorah and, according to scholar Carol Meyers, "this abundance of information clearly attests to the position of the menorah among the major appurtenances of the tabernacle and to its being an integral part of its ritual."[3]

Scholars have linked the image of John's vision with Zechariah 4:2, in which an angel points the prophet to a vision of a menorah, just as John's attention on Patmos is directed to the seven lampstands. The context of Zechariah's vision deals with the temple and its reconstruction under Zerubbabel. "Insofar as Zechariah's visions are related to the Jerusalem temple, the appearance of a golden lampstand or menorah surely involves a major temple appurtenance."⁴ Thus, the common linkage of Revelation 1:12 to Zechariah 4:2 enforces the sanctuary background of the Revelation candlesticks.

Much speculation has existed in Jewish thought on the menorah, especially because the Old Testament describes only how the menorah was to be built and where it was to sit in the sanctuary, while never telling what it represented. Josephus tied it to the seven known planets.⁵ Other Jewish sources have linked the menorah to the seven days of creation.⁶ Christians have seen the lamp as symbolic of Jesus Himself.⁷ In Revelation, however, John is told by the angel that the seven lampstands "are the seven churches" (Revelation 1:20), which are to receive specific messages from the Lord.

What John sees, therefore, isn't a "heavenly counterpart of the seven-branched candlestick of the ancient earthly sanctuary."⁸ Instead, it's merely a symbol of the earthly churches. What's significant, however, is that the Lord used a sanctuary image to depict the churches. The New Testament writers often used the temple (sanctuary) as a symbol of the church itself (see Ephesians 2:21; 1 Peter 2:4, 5; and 1 Corinthians 3:16, 17).⁹ Thus, the first vision in Revelation begins with a reference to the sanctuary service.

John then is immediately shown one "like the Son of Man" (Revelation 1:13) walking among the candlesticks. This "Son of Man" is Jesus, as verses 11 and 18 make especially clear.¹⁰ Jesus is referred to more than eighty times in the New Testament as "the Son of Man." In this verse, however, the definite article does not appear in Greek, so it reads literally "one like *a* Son of Man." That phrase, without the article, is used for Jesus in two other places as well.¹¹ With or without the article, the title points to Christ, often with an emphasis on His human nature.¹²

The phrase "One like the Son of Man" (Revelation 1:13) is an exact translation of the Aramaic in Daniel 7:13,¹³ a description of the pre-advent judgment,¹⁴ a heavenly tribunal in which "*One like the Son of Man* . . . [came] with the clouds of heaven! He came to the Ancient of Days, and they brought Him near before Him" (Daniel 7:13, emphasis supplied). The link with Revelation 1:13 is obvious. "According to the promise contained in Daniel's vision," writes Robert Wall, "the 'one like a son of man,' will come on the clouds to receive 'sovereign power' from God as the authorized representative of God's people (Dan 7:27). John finds the fulfillment of Daniel's promise in Christ Jesus, who now stands among the lampstands, symbols for the 'true' Israel of God, as exalted Lord."[15]

Meanwhile, Daniel 7:13, a judgment scene, has powerful ties to the heavenly sanctuary,[16] although this first vision in Revelation does not depict judgment. Instead, it's merely borrowing Old Testament language, as John does heavily throughout Revelation.[17]

The "Son of Man" in Revelation 1:13 is dressed "with a garment down to the feet and girded about the chest with a golden band," vestures worn by the High Priest in the earthly sanctuary service. "The robe and the garb," writes G. B. Caird, "are the garb of the high priest."[18] "The garment worn by the one 'like a son of man,' recalls the vesture of the High Priest of the Hebrew cultus."[19] Many commentators link this garment to the one worn by the High Priest of the earthly sanctuary service, especially because in the Septuagint, an ancient Greek translation of the Hebrew Bible, the same Greek word used in Revelation for the "garment down to the feet" is used for the priest's robe in Exodus.[20] The breastplate worn by the High Priest also ties this scene to Christ's high-priestly ministry. "The high girding ('about the paps')," writes Robert Mounce, "denotes the dignity of an important office and suggests that this part of the description as well is intended to set forth the high priestly function of Christ."[21]

Not only, then, does the first vision in Revelation relate to the sanctuary; it ties Jesus to His role as High Priest. Jesus is not *shown* first as the Lamb who died for the sins of the world or as the Lion who returns with a sharp sword with which to "strike the nations" (Revelation 19:15). Instead, the first time Jesus *appears*—is actually seen—in Revelation, in vision, He appears as High Priest. This makes perfect sense, because the book of Hebrews clearly states that, after His death, Jesus began functioning as our High Priest in heaven. "Seeing then that we have a great High Priest who has passed through the heavens, Jesus the Son of God, let us hold fast our confession" (Hebrews 4:14). Hebrews tells about Jesus as High Priest; Revelation *shows* Him in that role.

Only by virtue of what Christ accomplished as the Lamb, does He function as High Priest. "For such a High Priest was fitting for us, who is holy, harmless, undefiled, separate from sinners, and has become higher than the heavens; who does not need daily, as those high priests, to offer up sacrifices, first for His own sins and then for the people's, for this He did once for all when He offered up Himself" (Hebrews 7:26, 27). Both roles are inseparable, which is probably why John *sees* Jesus as High Priest in the vision but immediately *hears* Jesus refer to His role as the Lamb. "Do not be afraid," Jesus said to John, who had fallen at His feet, "I am the First and the Last. I am He who lives, and was dead, and behold, I am alive forevermore. Amen. And I have the keys of Hades and of Death" (Revelation 1:17, 18).

By calling Himself "the First and the Last," Jesus uses a phrase directly from Isaiah 44:6. "Thus says the Lord, the King of Israel, and his Redeemer, the Lord of hosts: 'I am the First and I am the Last; Besides Me there is no God' " (Isaiah 44:6). Thus in Revelation, Jesus clearly proclaims His own divinity, and when He says, "I am He who lives," He uses another phrase that refers to divinity. "Joshua said, 'By this you shall know that the *living God* is among you' " (Joshua 3:10, emphasis supplied).

These references to Christ's sovereignty as God are immediately juxtaposed to His words "and was dead," or more literally, "and became dead," a reference to Christ's death on the cross as the "Lamb of God." Here is the essence of the good news, the almost incomprehensible truth that the One by whom "all things were created that are in heaven and that are on earth, visible and invisible" (Colossians 1:16), the Living God, died as a substitute for humanity. "But God demonstrates His own love toward us, in that while we were still sinners, Christ died for us"

(Romans 5:8). It seems that Jesus purposely emphasized His divinity, only to immediately contrast it with the cross. He was the "First and the Last," "the Living God"—and yet He died a sinner's death on behalf of humanity! It's the greatest truth of the universe!

Christ then says, "And, behold, I am alive forevermore" (verse 18), an obvious reference to His resurrection. Even though He died, Jesus is now alive and is working in behalf of His people. They never have to fear that He will be gone from them again. He is "alive forevermore."

Also, by virtue of His death and resurrection, Jesus assured the churches that He now has "the keys of Hades and of Death." Because of Christ's victory at the cross, and then His victory over the grave itself, His people no longer have to fear death. "Death and the grave, therefore," writes Beasly-Murray, "hold no terrors for Christ's people, nor need they fear those who have the power to inflict death and send them to the grave—an important reminder in the context of the book."[22]

Just as death was not able to hold Christ, it is unable to hold His people either, but only because of what He has done for them. "Inasmuch then as the children have partaken of flesh and blood, He Himself likewise shared in the same, that through death He might destroy him who had the power of death, that is, the devil" (Hebrews 2:14). "So when this corruptible has put on incorruption, and this mortal has put on immortality, then shall be brought to pass the saying that is written: *'Death is swallowed up in victory.' 'O death, where is your sting? O Hades, where is your victory?'* " (1 Corinthians 15:54, 55).

The first vision in Revelation, therefore, not only has a strong emphasis on the death and resurrection of Christ, but it unmistakably places Jesus in His role as High Priest. Both aspects of His work are found there, and both aspects are inseparably tied to the sanctuary.

Yet despite the sanctuary motif and the obvious view of Christ as a High Priest, Revelation, chapter 1 doesn't focus on heaven, nor is it a heavenly sanctuary scene. Instead, Jesus is seen in His high-priestly role, with the emphasis on His relationship to the earthly church, symbolized by the seven golden lampstands amid which Christ is walking. This vision shows that even though Jesus has ascended to heaven as our High Priest, He is still closely tied to His church on earth. "Lo, I am with you always, even to the end of the age" (Matthew 28:20). "I will never leave you nor forsake you" (Hebrews 13:5). "For where two or three are gathered together in My name, I am there in the midst of them" (Matthew 18:20). This first vision in the book of Revelation shows Jesus in the midst of the churches, walking among His people.

In the rest of the vision, John relays messages from Christ to the churches, which are facing trials, challenges, and temptations. Christ as High Priest walking among the candlesticks symbolizes His closeness and watch care for His people during these struggles,[23] and the knowledge of Christ's continuing presence would encourage the faithful.[24] As High Priest in the heavenly sanctuary, Christ is able to help His church. "Therefore, in all things He had to be made like His brethren, that He might be a merciful and faithful High Priest in things pertaining to God, to make propitiation for the sins of the people. For in that He Himself has suffered, being tempted, He is able to aid those who are tempted" (Hebrews 2:17, 18).

This first vision intimates what becomes decidedly more clear later in Revelation: that the relationship between heaven and earth is close and causal. Revelation shows not only a two-tier reality, heaven and earth, but that both tiers are intimately related. It's a motif that continues throughout Revelation, until the very end of the book, when Christ is said to "tabernacle" (Revelation 21:3) with His people in a new heaven and a new earth.

---

1. The word *menorah* is derived from the Hebrew word *nyr*, which probably meant "to burn" or "to flame." It is also related to *nar*, a common Hebrew word that means "lamp."

2. Many scholars have seen the connection. See Charles, 25; Ford, 382; Ladd, 32. Elisabeth Schussler Fiorenza, *Revelation: Vision of a Just World* (Minneapolis: Fortress Press, 1991), 52. "The seven lampstands recall the ten lampstands placed in the nave or outer room of Solomon's temple (1 Kings 7:48, 49)." Jonathan Paulien,

BETWEEN THE LAMB AND THE LION

Intertextuality, The Hebrew Cultus, and the Plot of Apocalypse, paper read at the Literary Criticism and the Apocalypse Consultation, Society of Biblical Literature, New Orleans, 18 November 1990, 4.

3. Carol Meyers, *The Tabernacle Menorah* (Missoula, Mont.: Scholars Press, 1976), 17.

4. Carol Meyers and Eric Meyers, *Haggai, Zechariah 1-8*, The Anchor Bible (Garden City, N.Y.: Doubleday and Company, 1984), 1987.

5. Josephus, *Antiquities*, iii. 6.7. Quoted in Charles, 12.

6. "Symbolically the menorah represented the creation of the universe in seven days, the center light symbolizing the Sabbath. The seven branches are the seven continents of the earth and the seven heavens, guided by the light of God" *(The Jewish Encyclopedia*, s.v. "menorah."

7. "We search in vain for windows, only to find that sunbeams never play upon the sacred table nor does moonlight fall upon the golden altar. Only the candlesticks' seven flames chase the darkness from the chamber. . . . The lamp of life is Christ, man's only and complete everlasting light" (Leslie Hardinge, *With Jesus in His Sanctuary* [Harrisburg, Pa.: American Cassette Ministries, 1991], 147).

8. *SDA Bible Commentary*, 7:738.

9. See R. J. Mckelvey, *The New Temple: The Church in the New Testament* (New York: Oxford University Press, 1969), 92-132.

10. "I am the Alpha and the Omega, the First and the Last" (verse 11). "I am He who lives, and was dead, and behold, I am alive forevermore. Amen. And I have the keys of Hades and of Death" (verse 18).

11. Though many translations use the definite article, it doesn't appear in the Greek of these two verses: The Father "has given Him [the Son] authority to execute judgment also, because He is the Son of Man" (John 5:27). "I looked, and behold, a white cloud, and on the cloud sat One like the Son of Man, having on His head a golden crown, and in His hand a sharp sickle" (Revelation 14:14).

12. "Later the 'Son of man' became a fixed messianic expression to designate the heavenly Savior; and it was Jesus' favorite title to designate his own person and mission. The present reference goes back directly to Daniel, and serves not so much to designate Jesus as the heavenly king as to point out that while he is like a man, he is not merely a man; he is a supernatural being" (Ladd, 32).

13. In Daniel 7:13, the phrase is *kebar 'enash*.

14. See William Shea, *Selected Studies on Prophetic Interpretation* (Washington, D.C.: General Conference of Seventh-day Adventists, 1982), 94-123. Clifford Goldstein, *1844 Made Simple* (Boise, Idaho:

Pacific Press, 1988). Arthur Ferch, *The Son of Man in Daniel Seven*, Andrews University Seminary Doctrinal Dissertation Series, vol. 6 (Berrien Springs, Mich.: Andrews University Press, 1979), 145-154.

15. Robert Wall, *Revelation*, New International Biblical Commentary (Peabody, Mass.: Hendrickson Publishers, 1991), 62.

16. Though sanctuary imagery is not specifically mentioned in the judgment scene in Daniel 7, that scene does parallel the cleansing of the sanctuary in Daniel 8:14. Daniel 7:13 and Daniel 8:14 are two different ways of describing the same event. See Clifford Goldstein, *1844 Made Simple* (Boise, Idaho: Pacific Press, 1988). William Shea, "Unity of Daniel," in *Symposium on Daniel*, Frank Holbrook, ed. (Washington, D.C.: Biblical Research Institute, 1986), 165-220. Norman Gulley, "Daniel's Pre-Advent Judgment in Its Biblical Context," *Journal of the Adventist Theological Society* 2:2 (1991), 35-66.

"The coming of Christ as our high priest to the most holy place, for the cleansing of the sanctuary, brought to view in Daniel 8:14; the coming of the Son of man to the Ancient of Days, as presented in Daniel 7:13; and the coming of the Lord to His temple, foretold by Malachi, are descriptions of the same event" *(The Great Controversy, 426).*

17. "It is estimated that at least 550 quotations from the Old Testament are found in the book of Revelation" (Louis Were, *The Certainty of the Three Angels's Messages* [Berrien Springs, Mich.: First Impressions, 1979], 57).

18. Caird, 25.

19. Paulien, 4.

20. See Exodus 28:4; 29:5.

21. Robert Mounce, *The Book of Revelation*, The New International Commentary on the New Testament (Grand Rapids, Mich.: William B. Eerdmans, 1977), 78.

22. Beasly-Murray, 68.

23. "Christ is spoken of as walking in the midst of the golden candlesticks. Thus is symbolized His relation to the churches. He is in constant communication with His people. He knows their true state. He observes their order, their piety, their devotion. Although He is high priest and mediator in the sanctuary above, yet He is represented as walking up and down in the midst of His churches on earth" *(The Acts of the Apostles, 586).*

24. "The essential truth is that as Christ stands among the seven golden lampstands, he stands ever in unbroken fellowship with the churches on earth, persecuted though they may be" (Ladd, 34).

Chapter
Four
THE LAMB WHO WAS SLAIN

J ohn's vision of Christ, dressed as High Priest among the lampstands, introduced the letters to the seven churches. This is the first of six major prophetic sequences in Revelation; each of these sequences, like the letters to the churches, begins with a "victorious introduction scene with a temple setting."[1] In other words, each prophetic section is introduced by a vision that uses sanctuary imagery. These introductory visions show that Revelation is structured around the sanctuary. As Revelation progresses, the imagery in these victorious introduction scenes progresses as well, until the book covers the entire sanctuary service. Through these introduction scenes, Revelation encompasses Christ's entire ministry as High Priest in the heavenly sanctuary. "The heavenly sanctuary," writes Mervyn Maxwell, "is a central pivot in the message of Revelation."[2]

Just as the first phase of the earthly sanctuary service involved the death of an animal, the first phase of the heavenly service involved the death of Jesus, "who does not need daily, as those high priests, to offer up sacrifices, first for His own sins and then for the people's, for this He did once for all when He offered up Himself" (Hebrews 7:27). Besides offering Himself as the sacrifice for sin, Jesus—in order to be High Priest—had to be resurrected as well. These two events preceded Christ's high-priestly ministry in heaven. Perhaps, for this reason, Revelation 1, including the "victorious introduction scene" (verses 12-20), explicitly deals with His death and resurrection.

38

"Nowhere else in the book," writes Dick Davidson, "is such a concentrated emphasis upon Christ's earthly death and resurrection to be found."[3] This first chapter talks about Jesus as the "firstborn from the dead," "the faithful witness" the one who "washed us from our sins in His own blood," the one who "was dead" and now is "alive forevermore" (see verses 5, 18). Only after these events can the next phase of the sanctuary service, the ministration of the High Priest in heaven, begin.

The next victorious sanctuary introduction scene, pictured in Revelation 4 and 5, happens in heaven. "After these things I looked, and behold, a door standing open *in heaven*. And the first voice which I heard was like a trumpet speaking with me, saying, 'Come up here, and I will show you things which must take place after this.' Immediately I was in the Spirit; and behold, a throne set *in heaven*, and One sat on the throne" (Revelation 4:1, 2, emphasis supplied).

Unlike the first vision in chapter 1, which had an earthly setting, this vision points John heavenward. A door is open in heaven, a voice from heaven calls him to "Come up here," and the first thing he sees is a throne "in heaven." The emphasis of these introduction scenes has now shifted from earthly to celestial images.

"This heavenly setting is, in fact, emphasized," writes Kenneth Strand, "by the double reference to 'heaven'—the open door 'in heaven' and the throne 'in heaven.' "[4]

In Revelation 4, the One sitting upon the throne had the colors of "a jasper and a sardius stone," while a rainbow around the throne had the color of "an emerald" (verse 3). Around the throne were "twenty-four elders" (verse 4), and John saw "seven lamps of fire burning before the throne, which are the seven Spirits of God" (verse 5). Before the throne, too, was "a sea of glass, like crystal. And in the midst of the throne, and around the throne, were four living creatures" (verse 6). Chapter 5 has a "Lamb who was slain" (verse 12) and which has by its "blood" redeemed many "out of every tribe and tongue and people and nation" (verse 9). In that vision, too, John sees the twenty-four elders fall down before the Lamb, "each having a harp, and golden bowls full of incense, which are the prayers of the saints" (verse 8). This vision is the introductory scene of the second major prophetic sequence in Revelation, the seven seals.

Though some elements in this scene are not explicitly drawn from the Hebrew sanctuary, some are—and the cumulative effect of the elements "does reflect," writes Jon Paulien, "a strong reminiscence of that sanctuary and its services."[5]

The word for "door," *thura*, in Revelation 4:1 appears many times in the Septuagint in direct reference to the sanctuary. "He shall lay his hand on the head of his offering, and kill it at *the door* of the tabernacle of meeting" (Leviticus 3:1).[6]

In Revelation 4:1 John hears a voice "like a trumpet." Trumpets were part of the ancient Hebrew sanctuary service. "Also in the day of your gladness, in your appointed feasts, and at the beginning of your months, you shall blow the trumpets over your burnt offerings and over the sacrifices of your peace offerings; and they shall be a memorial for you before your God: I am the Lord your God" (Numbers 10:10).

The three precious stones John saw around the throne in Revelation 4:3—jasper, sardius, and emerald—appear also on the breastplate of the High Priest. Thus, they have a tie to the sanctuary as well.

The "seven lamps [*lampades*] of fire burning before the throne, which are the seven Spirits of God" (Revelation 4:5) recall either the seven-branched candlestick of the first apartment in the wilderness tabernacle or the lampstands used in the nave of Solomon's temple, although the Septuagint uses a different word for lampstand, *luchnia. Luchnia* is the word used also in Revelation 1 for the lampstands amid which Christ walked. Nevertheless, the seven fires that burned on the lampstand in the Holy Place establish a link to the "seven lamps of fire" in Revelation 4.

One of the most powerful sanctuary motifs in this vision is that of "a Lamb as though it had been slain" (Revelation 5:6), an obvious reference to the death of Christ. As shown in chapter 2, Christ's death derives its meaning only from the sanctuary service and the lessons about salvation it conveyed. The symbol of a slain lamb is linked to the Passover ceremony (see 1 Corinthians 5:7; Exodus 12:5, 7). Once the children of Israel built the tabernacle, and later the temple, the Passover service centered around these structures.

Also, one of the foundation sacrifices of the temple ritual was the "continual burnt offering" (Exodus 29:42), known also as the "daily."[7] Every day, morning and evening, two lambs were sacrificed (see Exodus 29:39, 42). This "daily" sacrifice comprised the basic ministry of the sanctuary service and was, as all the other sacrifices, a symbol of Christ's death. Thus, the image of the slain lamb in Revelation 5 must be interpreted only in the context of the sanctuary, because only in that context can the death of Jesus and what it accomplished be understood.

In Revelation 5, the twenty-four elders sing a song to the Lamb, saying, " 'You are worthy to take the scroll, and to open its seals; for You were slain, and have redeemed us to God by Your blood' " (verse 9). Blood, especially in the context of redemption, is a powerful sanctuary image. All through the Old Testament sacrificial system, blood shed from the various animal sacrifices, including lambs, was the oil that greased the engine of the sanctuary service. In one way or another, whether with bulls, goats, lambs, or birds, in daily or yearly rituals, almost every atoning sacrifice for intentional or unintentional sins of priests, rulers, or common people involved blood.

Revelation 5 talks about the twenty-four elders having "golden bowls full of incense, which are the prayers of the saints" (verse 8). Incense, of course, was also part of the tabernacle (and later temple) ritual. It was part of the daily. Just as the sacrifices were offered every evening and morning, so also the priest placed incense on the altar of incense in the first apartment every evening and morning. "Aaron shall burn on it sweet *incense* every morning; when he tends the lamps, he shall burn *incense* on it. And when Aaron lights the lamps at twilight, he shall burn *incense* on it, a perpetual [daily] *incense* before the Lord throughout your generations" (Exodus 30:7, 8, emphasis supplied). In Luke's account of Zacharias and Elizabeth, he tells how Zacharias was then serving as a priest and, "according to the custom of the priesthood, his lot fell to burn *incense* when he went into the *temple of the Lord*" (Luke 1:9, emphasis supplied).

Psalm 141:2 establishes the link between incense, prayer, and the sanctuary even more strongly: "Let my *prayer* be set before You as *incense*, the lifting up of my hands as the *evening sacrifice*" (emphasis supplied).[8]

Despite the sanctuary imagery in Revelation 4 and 5, vigorous debate ensues in Adventism over what this imagery represents. The first sanctuary scene, in chapter 1, shows the closeness of Christ as High Priest in heaven to His churches on earth. What does the next scene say?

Some, seeing imagery in Revelation 4 and 5 that parallels the heavenly tribunal in Daniel 7, believe that these chapters represent the investigative judgment.[9] However, the fact that the sanctuary imagery in Revelation 4 and 5 belongs to the first, not the second, apartment argues against the concept of judgment, which is a second-apartment phenomenon. In fact, the judgment is not even mentioned in these chapters. With the exception of Revelation 6:10, which is a call for judgment to happen (it hasn't yet), judgment language doesn't appear until much later in the book of Revelation. Finally, the sanctuary in heaven as depicted in Revelation places the investigative judgment in the last half of the book, when the second apartment comes into view. Thus, the basic structure of Revelation works against the idea of the sanctuary imagery in chapters 4 and 5 representing the judgment.[10]

The Daniel and Revelation Committee of the General Conference, a group of the church's top scholars, believes that the best explanation of what is happening in these two chapters is that Revelation 4 and 5 depict the inauguration of the heavenly sanctuary. After the emphasis in Revelation, chapter 1 on the cross and Christ's sacrifice, the view shifts to the heavenly sanctuary, where Christ began His work as High Priest. Because of the imagery in these scenes, and because this is the first view of the heavenly sanctuary in Revelation, the committee suggests that these chapters represent inauguration, the antitype of the earthly sanctuary's inauguration.[11]

One thing is clear: this heavenly scene emphasizes the Holy Place. Though images of trumpets, a slain lamb, blood, and stones on the breastplate of the high priest are general sanctuary images, the "seven lamps of fire" and "the golden bowls of incense" are distinctly first-apartment items. Thus, the introductory scenes have now shifted not only from earth to the heavenly sanctuary, but specifically to the Holy Place of the heavenly sanctuary.

Axiomatic to any emphasis on the sanctuary, either the first or second apartment, either in heaven or on earth, has to be the preceding sacrifice. The same applies to the sanctuary scene in Revelation 4 and 5. "The central focus is on the consequences of the cross, one of which was the establishment of Christ's reign in the heavenly sanctuary."[12] In the first introductory scene, Christ was upon earth; He is now in the sanctuary in heaven, pictured as a "Lamb as though it had been slain" (Revelation 5:6). Despite the first-apartment background of this heavenly scenario, this introductory scene stresses what Christ had accomplished on earth, as the Lamb.

In chapter 4, the twenty-four elders worship the Creator: " 'You are worthy, O Lord, to receive glory and honor and power; For You created all things, and by Your will they exist and were created' " (Revelation 4:11). In chapter 5, they worship the Redeemer: "For You were slain, and have redeemed us to God by Your blood out of every tribe and tongue and people and nation" (Revelation 5:9). It's the work of Christ as Redeemer that sets the stage for the opening of the seven seals, the prophetic sequence of events that follows this introductory scene and that eventually leads to the culmination of the plan of redemption.

At first glance, however, the opening of the seven seals doesn't seem positive. One seal has someone taking "peace from the earth . . . that people should kill one another" (Revelation 6:4). Under another seal, power was given "over a fourth of the earth, to kill with sword, with hunger, with death, and by the beasts of the earth" (Revelation 6:8). Under another "there was a great earthquake; and the sun became black as sackcloth of hair, and the moon became like blood" (Revelation 6:12).

Is this the work that Christ accomplished as the slain Lamb?

In a sense, yes. Christ Himself warned about calamities that would precede His return, and the seals show what some of those calamities will be. Jesus foretold of wars, famines, pestilences, and earthquakes that would make the world groan until He returns. Scholars have even linked the seals of Revelation 6 with Christ's warnings in the Gospels about the end of the world,[13] events that He said "must happen" (Mark 13:7).

Why *must* they happen? Because they are all part of the great controversy, and only against that background can these calamities be understood. The great controversy shows that for the ultimate good of humankind, and even for the good of the universe, evil must be fully revealed for what it is, both before human beings and before the unfallen universe. Only then can it be eradicated and never arise again. "What do you conspire against the Lord? He will make an utter end of it. Affliction will not rise up a second time" (Nahum 1:9).[14]

Revelation 4 and 5 show, too, that however bad things might be on earth, the Lord Jesus, from the sanctuary in heaven, is still in control. Just as Daniel, chapters 2, 7, 8, and 11 depicted the inevitable rise of vicious and cruel powers that would persecute God's people, these prophecies also proved that the Lord still had dominion over the earth and that He would ultimately bring out the consummation of His eternal glorious kingdom.[15] Revelation 4 and 5 just give a more detailed glimpse than did Daniel of what's happening in heaven, the source of what happens on earth.

"What is done in the temple in heaven," writes Kenneth Strand, "is done for the benefit of God's people on earth, and therefore the heavenly activity portrayed in the victorious-introduction scenes finds an immediate counterpart in the forces released on earth in order to accomplish God's purposes for His people."[16]

Revelation 4 and 5 also show the unbreakable link between heaven and earth; these chapters show that events in heaven are tied to events on earth, especially in regard to salvation.

"The breaking of the seven seals," writes Ladd, "is preliminary to the actual opening of the book and the events of the end time. It pictures the forces that will be operative throughout history by which the redemptive and judicial purposes of God will be forwarded."[17] Beasly-Murray wrote that the "judgments of the seals are but the precursors of the salvation of the world."[18]

Unquestionably, the best news from this second sanctuary

scene is the centrality of the cross. The seals are precursors to the consummation of redemption; they must be opened before Christ's purposes are accomplished in the salvation of human beings; and they were opened only because Jesus, by virtue of His death, was worthy to open them. Thus, events in heaven, which affect earth, happen only because of the cross—which means that what happens on earth results from the cross as well!

Whatever calamities the seals have brought, or whatever sufferings are foretold in the rest of Revelation, the cross screams out—across the pages of Revelation, across the centuries, across heaven and earth—that the God who would suffer and die for us is a God of such love that He is worthy of our trust, praise, and obedience, no matter how painful the circumstances that may engulf us now as the great controversy continues.

The centrality of the cross in Revelation 4 and 5 reveals, too, that although the Lion of the tribe of Judah is in heaven, bathed in the worship of heavenly beings, He was the Lamb who was slain on earth. Though now reigning as King, Jesus once toiled as a servant; though now enjoying the praise of the living creatures, the elders, and the angels, Jesus was once "despised and rejected by men" (Isaiah 53:3). Whatever the sufferings of humankind under the seals, the Lamb has suffered as a human being, bearing the brunt of sin and suffering as no other human ever will. Whatever His exalted position in heaven, Christ achieved it only because of what He did on earth, when He "was led as a lamb to the slaughter," when He "was wounded for our transgressions," when He was "bruised for our iniquities," when He "was numbered with the transgressors," when He was "oppressed" and "afflicted," when He was "smitten by God, and afflicted," and when He was "cut off from the land of the living" (Isaiah 53:7, 5, 12, 4, 8).

Thus, with the glory of the cross reaching even into heaven, no wonder the heavenly beings in the first apartment of the celestial sanctuary exclaim, "Worthy is the Lamb who was slain!" (Revelation 5:12).

---

1. Kenneth Strand, "Victorious Introduction Scenes," in *Symposium*

on Revelation, 51-72.

2. C. Mervyn Maxwell, *God Cares* (Boise, Idaho: Pacific Press, 1985), 164.

3. Dick Davidson, "Sanctuary Typology," in *Symposium on Revelation*, 6:112.

4. Strand, "Victorious Introduction Scenes," 55.

5. Paulien, 5. I rely heavily on Jon Paulien's work in this area for the rest of this chapter.

6. See also Exodus 29:4, 11; Leviticus 1:3, 5; 1 Kings 6:31, 32, 34.

7. In Hebrew, the word is *tamid*.

8. "Let the members of every family bear in mind that they are closely allied to heaven. The Lord has a special interest in the families of His children here below. Angels offer the smoke of the fragrant incense for the praying saints" *(Child Guidance*, 519).

"The incense, ascending with the prayers of Israel, represents the merits and intercession of Christ, His perfect righteousness, which through faith is imputed to His people, and which can alone make the worship of sinful beings acceptable to God. Before the veil of the most holy place was an altar of perpetual intercession, before the holy, an altar of continual atonement. By blood and by incense God was to be approached—symbols pointing to the great Mediator, through whom sinners may approach Jehovah, and through whom alone mercy and salvation can be granted to the repentant, believing soul" *(Patriarchs and Prophets*, 353).

9. See Martin Weber, *Some Call It Heresy* (Hagerstown, Md.: Review and Herald, 1985), 78, 79. Alberto Treiyer, *The Day of Atonement and the Heavenly Judgment* (Siloam Springs, Ark.: Creation Enterprises International, 1992), 472-502.

10. For a detailed refutation of the idea of judgment in these two chapters, see Jon Paulien, "Seal and Trumpets," 209-211.

11. The inauguration theory comes from the position that because "the scene contains a thorough mix of imagery from nearly every aspect of the Hebrew cultus" (Paulien, "Seals and Trumpets," 187), and because the inauguration of the sanctuary was the only time (with the exception of the Day of Atonement) that the entire sanctuary service was involved, then chapters 4 and 5 must be the inauguration of the heavenly sanctuary.

The problem with this theory is the assumption that the throne brought to view in these chapters (Revelation 4:2, 4, 6, 9, 10; 5:1, 6, 7, 11, 13) is automatically tied to the second apartment of the sanctuary.

It could be, but it doesn't have to be. While this view works fairly well for Revelation 4 and 5 itself, what happens, for example, when the throne is brought to view later in Revelation in contexts that are assumed to still be first-apartment scenes? I propose another answer to this problem. It will be discussed in the footnotes of chapter 8.

12. Paulien, "Seals and Trumpets," 187.

13. Some scholars have linked the events of the seals with Christ's discourse in Matthew 24, Luke 21, and Mark 13. They believe that the seven seals reflect the substance of those discourses, especially the one in Mark. See Charles, 158.

14. After depicting the death of Christ on the cross, Ellen White wrote, "Satan was not then destroyed. The angels did not even then understand all that was involved in the great controversy. The principles at stake were to be more fully revealed. And for the sake of man, Satan's existence must be continued. Man as well as angels must see the contrast between the Prince of light and the prince of darkness. He must choose whom he will serve" *(The Desire of Ages*, 761).

15. "Then to Him was given dominion and glory and a kingdom, that all peoples, nations and languages should serve Him. His dominion is an everlasting dominion, which shall not pass away, and His kingdom the one which shall not be destroyed" (Daniel 7:14, 15).

16. Strand, 71.

17. Ladd, 95, 96.

18. Beasly-Murray, 129.

Chapter
Five
THE PRAYERS OF THE SAINTS

As we have seen, the second "victorious introduction scene" using sanctuary imagery (Revelation 4 and 5) appears immediately following the first prophetic sequence (the letters to the churches) in Revelation 2 and 3. Likewise, immediately after the second prophetic sequence (the unloosing of the seven seals in Revelation 6 and 7), the third "victorious introduction scene" using sanctuary imagery appears:

> I saw the seven angels who stand before God, and to them were given seven trumpets. Then another angel, having a golden censer, came and stood at the *altar*. And he was given much *incense*, that he should offer it with the prayers of all the saints upon the *golden altar* which was before the throne. And the smoke of the *incense*, with the prayers of the saints, ascended before God from the angel's hand. Then the angel took the censer, filled it with fire from the *altar*, and threw it to the earth. And there were noises, thunderings, lightnings, and an earthquake (Revelation 8:2-5, emphasis supplied).

Right after this scene, the judgments of the seven trumpets are poured out on the earth, which include the burning of a third of the trees and all the grass (see verse 7), a third of the sea turning into blood (see verse 8), and a plague of locusts (see 9:3). Like the unloosing of the seven seals before them, these judgments don't appear to be particularly positive. Yet like the seals, these judgments don't happen arbitrarily, either. They are unloosed on earth only after something happens in the heavenly sanctuary.

And what is happening in the heavenly sanctuary? Jesus, first the Lamb of God "who takes away the sin of the world" (John 1:29) and now a "High Priest forever according to the order of Melchizedek" (Hebrews 6:20), is ministering in the Holy Place in our behalf. Thus, Revelation again assures us that even amid these calamities, which are all part of the great controversy, the Lord Jesus reigns in the sanctuary above.[1]

This great truth, though clarified in Revelation, isn't limited to it. The book of Job also reveals heavenly activity with earthly consequences. "Now there was a day when the sons of God came to present themselves before the Lord, and Satan also came among them" (Job 1:6).

In this heavenly scene, when the Lord asks Satan where he is coming from, Satan replies, "From going to and fro on the earth, and from walking back and forth on it" (verse 7). The Lord points Satan to the earth, to His servant Job, whom He describes as "a blameless and upright man, one who fears God and shuns evil" (verse 8).

Satan responds that the only reason Job obeys God is because the Lord has "made a hedge around him, around his household, and around all that he has on every side" (verse 10) and that if the Lord were to hurt Job and his possessions, then Job would "curse You to Your face" (verse 11).

The Lord tells Satan, "Behold all that he has is in your power" (verse 12).

This heavenly debate has definite earthly repercussions. Job is overwhelmed with suffering, including the death of his children. The story then returns to heaven, to another encounter between the Lord, Satan, and "the sons of God," which results in even more suffering for Job (see Job 2:1-13).

The point is that Job's trials didn't come in an existentialist vacuum. They weren't the meaningless sufferings of a meaningless life upon a meaningless world in a meaningless universe. Job's trials had purpose, and that purpose can be understood only in the great controversy context. The book of Job shows how closely heaven and earth are connected and how what happens in the former affects the latter.

Of course, not everything that happens in heaven has such "negative" effects here. Some results are overtly positive from the beginning. At Pentecost, Christ's followers were gathered in an upper room in Jerusalem, where they received the outpouring of the Holy Spirit:

> Now when the Day of Pentecost had fully come, they were all with one accord in one place. And suddenly there came a sound from heaven, as of a rushing mighty wind, and it filled the whole house where they were sitting. Then there appeared to them divided tongues, as of fire, and one sat upon each of them. And they were all filled with the Holy Spirit and began to speak with other tongues, as the Spirit gave them utterance (Acts 2:1-4).

This outpouring, which would have such powerful consequences on earth, came directly from a heavenly event: Christ's ascension to His Father. "This Jesus God has raised up, of which we are all witnesses. Therefore being exalted to the right hand of God, and having received from the Father the promise of the Holy Spirit, He poured out this which you now see and hear" (Acts 2:32, 33).[2]

Unquestionably, one of the most powerful examples of heaven's effect upon earth is the judgment of Daniel 7. The chapter depicts almost the whole span of world history: Babylon, Media-Persia, Greece, and Rome (pagan and papal). It then shifts toward heaven, to the judgment:

> I watched till thrones were put in place, and the Ancient of Days was seated; His garment was white as snow, and the hair of His head was like pure wool. His throne was a fiery flame, its wheels a burning fire; A fiery stream issued and came forth from before Him. A thousand thousands ministered to Him; Ten thousand times ten thousand stood before Him. The court was seated, and the books were opened (Daniel 7:9, 10).

50

THE PRAYERS OF THE SAINTS

After this judgment, the saints possess the kingdom, and a new era of human history begins. "But the court shall be seated, and they shall take away his dominion, To consume and destroy it forever. Then the kingdom and dominion, And the greatness of the kingdoms under the whole heaven, Shall be given to the people, the saints of the Most High" (Daniel 7:26, 27). The ushering in of the Lord's kingdom, the consummation of Christ's saving activity for humanity, comes as a direct result of this heavenly judgment.

So it is clear that events in heaven directly affect events on earth. The third sanctuary scene in Revelation, like those before it, is the precursor to events on earth—in this case, the effects of the seven trumpets. Whatever the meaning of the trumpets (another hotly debated topic within Adventism), they come only as a result of activity in heaven. Even in the midst of the calamities caused on earth by the trumpets, the scene returns to heaven, to the "horns of the golden altar which is before God" (Revelation 9:13), from which a voice orders the sixth angel to " 'Release the four angels who are bound at the great river Euphrates' " (verse 14). As a result, they are released "to kill a third of mankind" (verse 15), obviously an event with serious repercussions on earth.

Finally, this third sanctuary introduction scene is clearly tied to the first apartment of the heavenly sanctuary. The previous Holy Place scene, Revelation 4 and 5, was a general view; this third scene focuses specifically on the altar of incense. As shown in the previous chapter, the incense was part of the *tamid*, the daily intercession of the priests in the first apartment, the Holy Place, on behalf of sinners.

Thus, in the first eight chapters of Revelation, the sanctuary imagery all relates to the first apartment. We see Christ—dressed in priestly garb—appearing among seven candlesticks; in another place "seven lamps of fire" burn (Revelation 4:5); in another, smoke rises from a "golden altar" of incense (Revelation 8:3, 4). This imagery, all connected with the first apartment, shows that Christ's activity in the heavenly sanctuary, at least in this part of the book of Revelation, must be in the first apartment too.

Some have even detected parallels between the first eight chapters of Revelation and the talmudic tractate *Tamid* (an ancient Jewish commentary on the Bible, c. fifth century A.D.) which "contains all the regulations for the offering of the regular daily sacrifices in accordance with Numbers 28:3, 4".[3] In other words, John's heavenly vision of the Holy Place (where the daily, or *tamid*, occurred in the earthly sanctuary) appears to be "subtly associated with the activities in the temple related to the continual or *tamid* service."[4]

Mishnah Tamid (3.9), for example, deals with the priests trimming the lampstand; Revelation 1:12-20 has Christ among the lampstands. *Mishnah Tamid* (3.7) has "a great gate" being opened; Revelation has a door open in heaven (see Revelation 4:1). *Mishnah Tamid* (3.7) has a lamb slain; so does Revelation 5:6. *Mishnah Tamid* (5.4) has the offering of incense; Revelation 8:3, 4 does as well. And, finally, *Mishnah Tamid* (7:3) has trumpets blowing; Revelation 8:1 has trumpets too.

Parallels obviously exist, even if they are not as many or as "striking" as some suggest.[5]

More importantly, however, if Hebrews identifies Jesus as our High Priest, interceding for us in the heavenly sanctuary, and if the first half of Revelation has the post-cross Christ in the first apartment of that sanctuary, what does that aspect of His work entail? On the Day of Atonement, the work in the first apartment continued (see Numbers 29:7-11), so salvation is an ongoing process, even for those living in the second phase of Jesus' heavenly ministry.

Yet the more important question is, What is Christ doing while ministering? What is this first-apartment ministry, and what does it mean that Christ intercedes for us there? And, even more important, How is this intercession related to what He accomplished at Calvary?

---

1. "One thing will certainly be understood from the study of Revelation—that the connection between God and His people is close and decided.

"A wonderful connection is seen between the universe of heaven and this world. The things revealed to Daniel were afterward complemented by the revelation made to John on the Isle of Patmos. These two books should be carefully studied" *(Testimonies to Ministers*, 114).

2. "Christ's ascension to heaven was the signal that His followers were to receive the promised blessing. For this they were to wait before they entered upon their work. When Christ passed within the heavenly gates, He was enthroned amidst the adoration of the angels. As soon as this ceremony was completed, the Holy Spirit descended upon the disciples in rich currents, and Christ was indeed glorified, even with the glory which He had with the Father from all eternity. The Pentecostal outpouring was Heaven's communication that the Redeemer's inauguration was accomplished. According to His promise, He had sent the Holy Spirit from heaven to His followers as a token that He had, as priest and king, received all authority in heaven and on earth, and was the Anointed One over His people" (*The Acts of the Apostles*, 38, 39).

3. Maurice Simon, "Introduction," *Tamid* (London: Soncino Press, 1948), ix.

4. Paulien, "Intertextuality," 13.

5. Paulien, for example, links Revelation 6:9, 10—in which the souls under the altar cry out for God to avenge their blood—to *Mishnah Tamid* 4.1, in which the priest pours out the leftover blood of the sacrifice on "the southern base of the altar." It's hard to see that parallel. Other discrepancies exist too. Nevertheless, while it might be too much to say that the first eight chapters of Revelation are "modeled on the continual *Tamid* services of the temple" ("Intertextuality," 12), a link does appear to exist. Some, however, reject the link altogether. "The literary structure of the first chapters of Revelation does not follow . . . the Rabbinic *tamid* as it was recently suggested" (Alberto Trieyer, *The Day of Atonement and the Heavenly Judgment* [Siloam Springs, Ark.: Creation Enterprise International, 1992], 671).

Chapter
Six

THE POST-CROSS CHRIST

Revelation begins with Christ's high-priestly ministry in the first apartment of the heavenly sanctuary. In the Old Testament earthly type, the first-apartment ministry involved intercession, with the priest manipulating animal blood either in the courtyard or in the sanctuary itself.

What, however, happens in New Testament times, when the High Priest is Jesus, when He's ministering in the heavenly sanctuary, and the blood is His own?

Just as the earthly priest's work in the sanctuary couldn't be separated from the sacrifice, neither can Christ's work in heaven be separated from His sacrifice. The heavenly ministry makes sense only in relation to the earthly. His work on earth, in fact, prepared Him for His work in heaven.

"Therefore, in all things He had to be made like His brethren, that He might be a merciful and faithful High Priest in things pertaining to God, to make propitiation for the sins of the people. For in that He Himself has suffered, being tempted, He is able to aid those who are tempted" (Hebrews 2:17, 18).

"For we do not have a High Priest who cannot sympathize with our weaknesses, but was in all points tempted as we are, yet without sin" (Hebrews 4:15).

"Though He was a Son, yet He learned obedience by the things which He suffered. And having been perfected, He became the author of eternal salvation to all who obey Him, called by God as High Priest 'according to the order of Melchizedek' " (Hebrews 5:8-10).

These verses imply that Christ's humanity didn't end with His earthly mission.[1] The humanity that Jesus appropriated at the incarnation He took to heaven; otherwise, if He had shed His humanity upon entering heaven, how could He still relate to human temptation?

"It is by his Ascension," writes Brian K. Donne, "that Christ has borne our humanity, which he assumed at the Incarnation, to the throne of the Godhead."[2]

What He experienced as the "Lamb of God," when He "learned obedience by the things which He suffered," are what now make Him "a merciful and faithful High Priest" able to help His redeemed in the "time of need." By virtue of His own ever-present humanity, Jesus can, as High Priest, remain close enough to deliver us from the temptations that He has already overcome.

No wonder the Bible says that "no temptation has overtaken you except such as is common to man; but God is faithful, who will not allow you to be tempted beyond what you are able, but with the temptation will also make the way of escape, that you may be able to bear it" (1 Corinthians 10:13). God can make a way of escape from temptation because God Himself overcame it.

Christ's humanity is His great link to us, the tie that binds Him to His redeemed in ways that He can never be bound to other parts of His creation. The post-cross Christ is still *the Son of man*. Just before death, Stephen gazed into the heavens, where he saw "*the Son of Man* standing at the right hand of God" (Acts 7:56, emphasis supplied.) Daniel, watching the pre-advent judgment, saw "one like *the Son of Man*" coming "with the clouds of heaven" (Daniel 7:13, emphasis supplied). This Son of man is now our High Priest. Thus, even amid the great trials of God's church, even amid the calamities that come upon the world, God's people have the surety, assurance, and promise that Jesus hasn't forsaken them, that He still has forever bound Himself to them with a closeness that reaches from heaven to earth!

"For both He who sanctifies and those who are being sanctified are all of one, for which reason He is not ashamed to call them brethren. . . . Inasmuch then as the children have partaken of flesh and blood, He Himself likewise shared in the same"

(Hebrews 2:11, 14).

The humanity that Jesus took while He did His work on the earth, the humanity that has linked Him to human flesh and blood, remains while He ministers in the heavenly sanctuary. A Man lives among the stars who understands hunger, thirst, exhaustion, and stress. "Christ has taken his humanity into the very presence of God," writes Baptist theologian Robert H. Culpepper. "This means that we may come with boldness into the presence of God, knowing that we have a high priest who is able to sympathize with us in our weaknesses."[3]

Light years away, a Man intercedes for us before God—a Man who has suffered in the flesh, who has heard the devil's whispers, who has felt the carnal scream, who has experienced the anguish of abuse, disappointment, and mistreatment. A Man who has been pulled by the tug of lust, pride, anger, selfishness, and hate, even if, unlike us, He succumbed to none.

"Since He has experienced the suffering of being tempted in every respect as we are," writes Culpepper, "He is able to sympathize with us fully in our weakness. The fact that He came through without sin makes Him no less able to identify with us. Rather it gives to Him a sensitivity which sin would have deadened. Moreover, 'His successful conflict carries with it the right to represent, to help, to save.' "[4]

Yet Jesus had to become us to save us, not just from sinning, but from the legal consequences of sin itself. What good would victory or a moral and holy life be if we were ultimately lost? Christianity has to be more than ethics, morality, and behavior, because ethics, morality, and behavior aren't enough for salvation. Christ must be doing more than just giving us holy lives or delivering us from temptation. Victory alone isn't enough, because salvation is more than obedience. Obedience by itself, even that which comes from a relationship with Christ, can procure nothing but works, which in and of themselves aren't salvific.

"Now to him who works, the wages are not counted as grace but as debt. But to him who does not work, but believes on Him who justifies the ungodly, his faith is accounted for righteousness" (Romans 4:4, 5).

The most important aspect of Christ's work in heaven merely

extends the most important aspect of His work on earth—atonement. In the fullest, truest sense of the *atonement* (not the limited view among some evangelicals), Christ's high-priestly ministry is as much a part of the atonement as was His death on the cross. The two can't be separated, any more than the death of the animal in the earthly sanctuary could be separated from the ministration of its blood by the priest.

"Moreover," writes Donne, "His perpetual intercession is no less needful for our acceptance than was His death on Calvary, because His presence before the Father is the standing guarantee of our being presented and accepted in heaven (cf. Heb. 9:24; 7:24f)."[5] Though performing different functions and different roles, Christ's work on earth and His work in heaven are inseparable. What He is doing as our Intercessor is another phase of what He completed as our Sacrifice.[6]

"The fundamental point to remember," writes L. Berkhof, "is that the ministry of intercession should not be dissociated from the atonement, since they are but two aspects of the same redemptive work of Christ, and the two may be said to merge into one. Martin finds that the two constantly appear in juxtaposition and are so closely related in Scripture that he feels justified in making the following statement: 'The essence of Intercession is Atonement; and the Atonement is essentially an Intercession.' "[7]

No doubt Jesus Christ paid the complete penalty for sin at the cross. His perfect life was the only life needed, the only life sufficient, the only life good enough to redeem humankind from the wages of sin. By His sacrifice the demands of the law, the demands of righteousness, the demands of a holy God were fully met and fully answered. After Calvary, all sinful humanity had the opportunity to stand accepted by the Father, thanks only to Jesus, whose perfection and holiness have been made available to every human being. Because of what Christ finished at the cross, He freely offers each of us eternal life instead of eternal destruction, pardon instead of condemnation, blessings instead of curses, reconciliation instead of estrangement, and a robe of perfection woven on the loom of heaven instead of filthy garments defiled on earth. Nothing any of us can do either adds or takes away from the cross. Though Calvary stands at the center of human history, it also stands above it, complete in itself, immutable, ever-valid, ever-sufficient, and ever-available—the essence of God's work on humanity's behalf.

In this sense, atonement was complete at the cross—a work done outside of us, independent of us, yet ultimately for us. Still, the Bible is clear that Christ is doing another work *for us* even now, long after His death.

"Who is he who condemns? It is Christ who died, and furthermore is also risen, who is even at the right hand of God, who also makes intercession *for us*" (Romans 8:34, emphasis supplied).

"Therefore He is also able to save to the uttermost those who come to God through Him, since He ever lives to make intercession *for them*" (Hebrews 7:25, emphasis supplied).

"Where the forerunner has entered *for us*, even Jesus, having become High Priest forever according to the order of Melchizedek" (Hebrews 6:20, emphasis supplied).

"For Christ has not entered the holy places made with hands, which are copies of the true, but into heaven itself, now to appear in the presence of God *for us*" (Hebrews 9:24, emphasis supplied).

"He poured out His soul unto death, And He was numbered with the transgressors, and He bore the sin of many, and made intercession *for the transgressors*" (Isaiah 53:12, emphasis supplied).

Obviously, despite what Christ finished at Calvary, He's still working for us; otherwise, Romans, Hebrews, and Isaiah wouldn't talk about Christ's intercession.

This truth is one of the great, and often neglected, aspects of the plan of salvation. As one evangelical writes: "Several years ago a number of writers voiced concern that attention to the present work of Christ has been 'largely neglected' by the systematic theologians of the church. The authors of the New Testament would not have understood such neglect, for Christ's present work is one of their most important themes."[8]

Of course, "the present work of Christ" in the heavenly sanctuary has also been one of the "most important themes" for

Seventh-day Adventists for more than a century.

What exactly does it entail?

After our first parents sinned, they would not directly confess. Instead, both tried to put the blame elsewhere. So quickly had their natures and characters changed from those of perfect sinless beings into those of sinners that they immediately started to appropriate some traits of Satan, the father of lies.

With the fall of Adam and Eve, all their descendants took that same character and nature as well, and soon the whole world was filled with beings naturally corrupted, fallen, and evil. "Then the Lord saw that the wickedness of man was great in the earth; and that every intent of the thoughts of his heart was only evil continually" (Genesis 6:5). The apostle Paul, commenting on the condition of human beings, quoted Scripture when he wrote: "There is none righteous, no not one" (Romans 3:10).

The theological phrase for humans' condition is "total depravity." This doesn't mean that human beings are absolutely evil and perverted, but rather that every aspect of our essence is infected by sin and that no part of us has escaped its corruption. "There is no limit or boundary within human nature," writes G. C. Berkhouwer, "beyond which we can find some last human reserve untouched by sin; it is man himself who is totally corrupt."[9]

When Isaiah wrote that all our righteousness is as "filthy rags" (Isaiah 64:6), he used the words *beged idiym*, which mean "a garment defiled by menstruation." If our *righteousness* is like a *beged idiym*, what are our selfishness, envy, greed, lust, and hatred?

Satan caused our first parents' fall by enticing them away from their Maker. He has successfully employed that tactic ever since, luring people away from God by pointing them to temptations of the world, which is why he's called "the god of this age" (2 Corinthians 4:4). He tried the same with Jesus in the wilderness and failed, but it has worked with almost everyone else. Of course, some in every age have looked "for the city which has foundations, whose builder and maker is God" (Hebrews 11:10); they have confessed "that they were strangers and pilgrims on the earth" (verse 13); and that they "desire a better, that is, a heavenly country" (verse 16). But these are the exceptions; the rule is that Satan "deceives the whole world" (Revelation 12:9), and his most powerful ploy for that deception is to kindle in people a love of the world instead of, or simply greater than, a love of God.

"Adulterers and adulteresses! Do you not know that friendship with the world is enmity with God? Whoever therefore wants to be a friend of the world makes himself *an enemy of God*" (James 4:4, emphasis supplied).

"For to be carnally minded is death, but to be spiritually minded is life and peace. Because the carnal mind *is enmity against God*" (Romans 8:6, 7, emphasis supplied).

"This I say, therefore, and testify in the Lord, that you should no longer walk as the rest of the Gentiles walk, in the futility of their mind, having their understanding darkened, *being alienated from the life of God*, because of the ignorance that is in them" (Ephesians 4:17, 18, emphasis supplied).

Karl Marx, in his *Economic and Philosophical Manuscripts of 1844* (that's the date!) wrote that the essence of people's problem was that they were being alienated by the capitalistic economy in which they were enslaved. Marx used the biblical account of the fall and humanity's subsequent alienation from God as his metaphor for reality. Ironically, Marx's metaphor, not his reality, is the literal truth: people's alienation doesn't come because of what they do from nine to five, but from sin, which has alienated them from their Creator, the source of their existence, essence, and purpose.

Why? Because God "is holy, holy, holy" (Revelation 4:8) and we are sinful, sinful, sinful. Because God's ways are "just and true" (Revelation 15:3), and ours are unjust and false. Because God is "righteous," and we are like *beged idiym*. Because God is perfect, and we are imperfect; He is merciful, and we are merciless; He is forgiving, and we are condemning; and He is selfless while we are selfish. "Because your iniquities have separated you from your God; and your sins have hidden His face from you, So that He will not hear" (Isaiah 59:2).

"In the biblical view," writes Raoul Dederen, "there is a fundamental hostility between unregenerate man and his Creator. Sin brought it about. Sin broke the fellowship and created a barrier between man and God, not to mention man and man."[10]

Sin is the antithesis of God. It stands in opposition to all that God is. God is holy, perfect, righteous, and sin is none of these. In fact, it's their opposite. And, because we are sinful by nature, we are naturally in opposition to God and at enmity with all that He is.

God's love of humanity, however, is greater than His revulsion against sin. As much as His perfection and righteousness might demand that sin be destroyed, His love demands that people be saved. God wants to eradicate sin, not sinners. He is "not willing that any should perish but that all should come to repentance" (2 Peter 3:9). "It is not the will of your Father who is in heaven that one of these little ones should perish" (Matthew 18:14).

Because sin is a problem to God and human beings, Jesus, the God-man, solved it for both at the cross. For human beings, Jesus paid the penalty for the sins that otherwise would lead to their eternal death. "Christ has redeemed us from the curse of the law, having become a curse for us" (Galatians 3:13). And for God, His judgment against sin was poured out upon Jesus, not upon us, so that we could be saved from the condemnation that sin must ultimately bring. "God demonstrates His own love toward us, in that while were still sinners, Christ died for us" (Romans 5:8).

At the cross, God's revulsion against sin and His love for humanity reached their climax; the great paradox of God's hatred of sin and His love for sinners was resolved; and God was able to bridge the gulf between Himself and humanity caused by sin.

"For if when we were enemies we were *reconciled* to God through the death of His Son, much more, having been *reconciled*, we shall be saved by His life. And not only that, but we also rejoice in God through our Lord Jesus Christ, through whom we have now received the *reconciliation*" (Romans 5:10, 11, emphasis supplied).

"Wherefore in all things it behoved him to be made like unto his brethren, that he might be a merciful and faithful high priest in things pertaining to God, to make *reconciliation* for the sins of the people" (Hebrews 2:17, KJV, emphasis supplied).

"For it pleased the Father that in Him all the fullness should dwell, and by Him to *reconcile* all things to Himself, by Him, whether things on earth or things in heaven, having made peace through the blood of His cross" (Colossians 1:19, 20, emphasis supplied).

Sin has caused humans to be at enmity with God, alienated and separated from Him. Christ, however, has reconciled humans and God by bearing the full brunt of God's wrath against sin at Calvary. "Now is the judgment of this world," Jesus said (John 12:31), just before His death. The world was sinful and deserved the full punishment of sin; instead, Christ, out of love for humankind, took that punishment upon Himself, "being made a curse for us," so we don't have to face the condemnation that our sins would otherwise bring.

Thus, not only did Jesus bear the brunt of our sins, paying with His life what we deserved from ours, but His perfect sinless life stands in place of our imperfect sinful one. Though we are sinners and have broken God's law, alienating ourselves from God, Christ stands in our stead, and the perfection and righteousness wrought out in His life are credited to ours. We are accepted by God, not on the basis of our own righteousness, which is as *beged idiym*, but on the basis of His righteousness, which we acquire by faith. When we are "in Christ Jesus," God sees us as He sees Jesus, and we are justified, forgiven, and reconciled to God because of the righteousness of Christ.

Here is reconciliation. It comes only because of God's saving act for humanity. "God was in Christ, *reconciling the world to Himself*, not imputing their trespasses to them" (2 Corinthians 5:19, emphasis supplied). We are reconciled because our sin, which has caused the alienation, is no longer imputed, or credited, to us; it all fell on Jesus at the cross. Though God through Christ has reconciled the world to Himself, only those who avail themselves of that reconciliation enjoy union with God through Christ so "that they may all be one, as You, Father, are in Me, and I in You; that they also may be one in Us" (John 17:21), a union that gives us eternal life.

Through the atoning death of Jesus, fallen men and women can stand reconciled to God. By His grace, God has chosen to view us, not as we truly are in all our imperfection, but as Christ is in all His perfection. Instead of leaving us to face the legal consequences of our sins, the Lord made Jesus "who knew no sin to be sin for us, that we might become the righteousness of God in Him" (2 Corinthians 5:21). We come to Calvary broken-hearted and converted, and God, instead of seeing our sin, evil, and depravity, sees the holiness and perfection of Jesus. Here is the only way the sinner can be justified, reconciled, and unified with God. This reconciliation comes from the cross, from the work that Jesus finished for us almost two thousand years ago.

Of course, the good news is not only that God forgives us our sins because of Christ, but that He promises to give us victory over them as well. Yet even with all the Bible promises about being victorious (see 1 Corinthians 10:13), being dead to sin (see Romans 6:2, 11), overcoming the world (see 1 John 5:4), becoming a new creation in Christ (see 2 Corinthians 5:17), Christ being formed in us (see 2 Corinthians 4:10, 11), partaking of the divine nature (see 2 Peter 1:4), being perfect (see Matthew 5:48), living by the Spirit (see Romans 8:9-13), crucifying the flesh (see Galatians 5:24), being obedient (see 1 Peter 1:14), having pure thoughts (see 2 Corinthians 10:5), and keeping the commandments (see 1 John 5:2)—Christians still sin!

We shouldn't. We have the Creator of the universe promising power to overcome. "That same powerful word," wrote A.T. Jones, "is to hold up the Christians in the Christians's course, precisely the same as it holds the sun in its course. The Christian who will put his confidence upon that word that is to hold him up, as he puts his confidence in that word that holds up the sun, will find that word will hold him up as it holds up the sun."[11] Yet, even with all that promised power—we still fall (as Jones' later apostasy amply proves).

The fault, of course, is not with God, His Word, or His promises, but with us, our choices, our carnal minds, and corrupt hearts. Sin—though it doesn't have to be—is still a personal reality for born-again, converted Christians who love God with all their hearts, souls, and minds. It was for Moses; it was for David; it was for Peter; it was for Ellen White; and it is for us too.

What happens when Christians sin? Paul wrote that through Christ's blood, the Lord could "demonstrate His righteousness, because in His forbearance God had passed over the sins *that were previously committed*" (Romans 3:25, emphasis supplied).

But what about the sins that are present, or even future?

"My little children, these things I write to you that you may not sin. And if anyone sins, we have an Advocate with the Father, Jesus Christ the righteous" (1 John 2:1).

John is talking to believers. Though admonishing them against sin, he's aware of its reality even among Christians, so he points them to Jesus, our Advocate, our High Priest, in the heavenly sanctuary.

Sin, which originally caused the rift between God and humanity, still does. It is no less heinous now than when Adam and Eve fell. "And every transgression and disobedience received a just reward" (Hebrews 2:2). Sins committed by Christians—maybe *especially* those committed by Christians—are an offense to God and must be dealt with.

Fortunately, for repentant Christians, Jesus lives as their Intercessor. "Therefore He is also able to save to the uttermost those who come to God through Him, since He ever lives to make intercession for them" (Hebrews 7:25).

By His intercession, Jesus stands between the sinner and God, just as did the priest in the earthly service. The priest entered the presence of God with the blood of an animal, which was accepted on behalf of the sinner, just as Jesus stands in the presence of God with His own blood, which is accepted in our stead. Christ, as Intercessor, is presenting His own blood, His own merits, before the Father, because there is nothing else.

Jesus is "the Mediator of the new covenant, and . . . the blood of sprinkling, that speaks better things than that of Abel" (Hebrews 12:24).

"Not with the blood of goats and calves, but with His own blood He [Jesus] entered the Most Holy Place once for all, having obtained eternal redemption" (Hebrews 9:12).

"Therefore, brethren, having boldness to enter the Holiest by the blood of Jesus" (Hebrews 10:19).

"The blood of Christ," writes Edward Heppenstall, "is heaven's currency. The repentant sinner cannot appeal to anything else, for nothing else is available. Before God, men can plead only the merits of Christ's sinless life and His perfect sacrifice. The believer has nothing to offer in himself."[12]

The born-again Christian is justified by faith in Christ (see Romans 5:1). Her faith is accounted as righteousness before God, who accepts the perfection of Christ in her stead (see Romans 4:5). When, however, she sins, and then confesses her sins, Christ, as her Advocate, stands before the Father, presenting His merits, holiness, and perfection, which are accepted in her stead. Thus, when God looks down upon the sinner, He doesn't see her in all her unrighteousness; He sees Jesus in all His holiness and perfection, presenting His merits on her behalf.

What are those merits? Jesus Himself possesses all the characteristics of the Father. Jesus is "the express image of His [the Father's] person" (Hebrews 1:3). Jesus Himself said, "He who has seen Me has seen the Father" (John 14:9). "I and my Father," Jesus said, "are one" (John 10:30).

Thus, the rift that sin causes between humans and God is continually being healed, not by humans, but by the intercession of Jesus, who constantly presents before the Father, not our shortcomings, but His own sinless perfection.

Here is the essence of Christ's atoning ministry in the heavenly sanctuary. Far from taking away from the cross, Christ's work in heaven is the constant *application* of the cross on behalf of born-again sinners, who always need to be covered by Christ's righteousness.

"Christ's continuous intercession for us," writes Culpepper, "is a constant reminder to us that God deals with us not on the basis of who we are or what we have done but on the merits of who Christ is and what He has done."[13]

Through Christ's high-priestly ministry, His work of justification and sanctification is constantly made available to those who by faith have accepted His death. As High Priest, Christ offers to believers not just a legal covering, but a personal experience of which they can partake. Because we have a High Priest who was "in all points tempted as we are, yet without sin" (Hebrew 4:15), we have the promise that Christ is working to give us the victories that He has already won for us. "But thanks be to God, who gives us the victory through our Lord Christ Jesus" (1 Corinthians 15:57).

Though these promises are real, available only through the work of Christ as our High Priest, we don't always avail ourselves of them, which is why we fall. And because we fall, we must have Jesus as our substitute and surety, standing between us and God.

Thus, when Revelation depicts Jesus as priest or shows the lampstand and the altar of incense in the first apartment of the heavenly sanctuary, we are being brought into the center of Christ's work in heaven. Despite the trials of the seven churches, the calamities of the seals, and the turmoil of the trumpets, the Christian has the hope, the promise, the comfort of knowing that Christ is his personal intercessor with the Father. Revelation shows that Christ has brought our humanity into the portals of heaven itself.

Therefore, no temptation is so great that Christ as Lamb hasn't overcome it or for which Christ as High Priest can't make a way of escape. No sin is so evil that Christ as Lamb has not fully paid for it or that Christ as High Priest cannot cover if we claim His merits. Every aspect of our salvation, completed by Jesus as a "Lamb as though it had been slain" (Revelation 5:6), is always, every moment, made available to His people by Jesus as "the Son of Man, clothed with a garment down to the feet and girded about the chest with a golden band" (Revelation 1:13).

---

1. "Christ ascended to heaven, bearing a sanctified, holy humanity. He took this humanity with Him into the heavenly courts, and through the eternal ages He will bear it, as the One who has redeemed every human being in the city of God, the One who has pleaded before the Father, 'I have graven them upon the palms of my hands'" *(SDA Bible Commentary*, 5:1125).

"Christ was to identify Himself with the interests and needs of humanity. He who was one with God has linked Himself with the children of men by ties that are never to be broken. Jesus is 'not ashamed to call them brethren' (Hebrews 2:11). He is our Sacrifice, our Advocate, our Brother, bearing our human form before the Father's throne, and through eternal ages one with the race He has redeemed—the Son of man" *(Steps to Christ*, 14).

"Although Jesus Christ has passed into the heavens, there is still a living chain binding His believing ones to His heart of infinite love. The most lowly and weak are bound by a chain of sympathy closely to His heart. He never forgets that He is our representative, that He bears our nature" *(Testimonies to Ministers*, 19).

2. Rev. Brian K. Donne, "The Significance of the Ascension of Jesus Christ in the New Testament," *Scottish Journal of Theology* 30 (1977), 564.

3. Robert H. Culpepper, "The High Priesthood and Sacrifice of Christ in the Epistle to the Hebrews," *The Theological Educator* 32 (1985), 54.

4. Ibid., 48.

5. Donne, 565.

6. "The intercession of Christ in man's behalf in the sanctuary above is as essential to the plan of salvation as was His death upon the cross. By His death He began that work which after His resurrection He ascended to complete in heaven" *(The Great Controversy*, 489).

7. L. Berkhof, *Systematic Theology* (Grand Rapids, Mich.: Eerdmans, 1949), 402.

8. David J. Macleod, *Bibliotheca Sacra*, 148 (April-June 1991), 184.

9. G. C. Berkhouwer, *Man, The Image of God* (Grand Rapids, Mich.: Eerdmans, 1962), 135.

10. Raoul Dederen, "Atoning Aspects in Christ's Death," in *The Sanctuary and the Atonement*, 300.

11. A. T. Jones, "Sermon No. 12," in *The Third Angel's Message* (Calistoga, Calif.: John Ford, Md., 1977), 218.

12. Edward Heppenstall, *Our High Priest* (Washington, D.C.: Review and Herald, 1972), 58, 59.

13. Culpepper, 58.

"Christ is the connecting link between God and man. He has promised His personal intercession. He places the whole virtue of His righteousness on the side of the suppliant. He pleads for man, and man, in need of divine help, pleads for himself in the presence of God, using the influence of the One who gave His life for the life of the world" *(Testimonies for the Church*, 8:178).

"By His spotless life, His obedience, His death on the cross of Calvary, Christ interceded for the lost race. And now, not as a mere petitioner does the Captain of our salvation intercede for us, but as a Conqueror claiming His victory. His offering is complete, and as our Intercessor, He executes His self-appointed work, holding before God the censer containing His own spotless merits and the prayers, confessions, and thanksgiving of His people" (*Christ's Object Lessons*, 156).

"As our Intercessor, His office work is to introduce us to God as His sons and daughters. Christ intercedes in behalf of those who have received Him. To them He gives power, by virtue of His own merits, to become members of the royal family, children of the heavenly King" (*In Heavenly Places*, 77).

"The religious services, the prayers, the praise, the penitent confession of sin ascend from true believers as incense to the heavenly sanctuary; but passing through the corrupt channels of humanity, they are so defiled that unless purified by blood, they can never be of value with God. They ascend not in spotless purity, and unless the Intercessor who is at God's right hand presents and purifies all by His righteousness, it is not acceptable to God. All incense from earthly tabernacles must be moist with the cleansing drops of the blood of Christ. He holds before the Father the censer of His own merits, in which there is no taint of earthly corruption. He gathers into this censer the prayers, the praise, and the confessions of His people, and with these He puts His own spotless righteousness. Then, perfumed with the merits of Christ's propitiation, the incense comes up before God wholly and entirely acceptable" (*That I May Know Him*, 75).

"How thankful we should be that we have a heavenly intercessor. Jesus presents us to the Father robed in his righteousness. He pleads before the Father in our behalf. He says, 'I have taken the sinner's place. Look not upon this wayward child, but look on me. Look not upon his filthy garments, but look on my righteousness' " (*Bible Echo and Signs of the Times*, 1 June 1882).

Chapter
Seven
THE ALTAR OF INCENSE

C hrist's high-priestly ministry, and the good news it entails, leads to another question. Is there a real edifice in heaven where Christ has been for the past two thousand years and, if so—what's in it?

The third sanctuary scene in Revelation, for example, shows an altar of incense. Does an altar exist in heaven, where an angel burns incense mixed with the prayers of God's people on earth?

How much in Revelation is real, and how much is symbolic? Are there living creatures in heaven full of eyes (see Revelation 4:8); are there a "door" (see verse 1) and "seven lamps of fire" (see verse 5)?

When Revelation describes the souls of the martyrs crying for vengeance (see Revelation 6:9, 10) or depicts a pregnant woman about to give birth in heaven (see verses 1, 2) or tells of a "great, fiery red dragon" whose tail threw down a third of the stars of heaven (see verses 3, 4), these images certainly aren't literal. When, therefore, Revelation shows sanctuary introduction scenes—are altars, incense, censers, and candlesticks tangible objects existing in heaven? Or are they symbols? And does it even matter?

It matters, but only to a point, because the real question is not whether beasts, covered all over with eyes, exist in heaven, but whether a sanctuary does. After the Millerite disappointment, those who clung to the basic prophetic numbers (after revising the prophetic events) founded the Seventh-day

Adventist Church on the assumption that a literal heavenly sanctuary existed. The sanctuary was their answer to the Millerite mistake.[1] If no heavenly sanctuary exists, their answer was wrong, and the S.D.A. Church has been established on a lie.

"The Seventh-day Adventist pioneers," writes P. Gerard Damsteegt, "never doubted the existence of an actual physical structure of a bipartite heavenly sanctuary. The Mosaic tabernacle was its counterpart on earth. Their sanctuary doctrine depended on its objective reality. They realized that without it there was no justification for their positions on Daniel 8:14 and the change in Christ's high priestly ministry on October 22, 1844."[2]

Adventism has always been plagued by those who concluded that there is no sanctuary in heaven. If valid, this challenge would be a dagger in the heart of Seventh-day Adventist doctrine. The church has been warned that it would face this attack, and it has.[3]

If the only biblical book we had were Revelation, the case for a literal sanctuary would be difficult. Revelation is, after all, overloaded with symbolism. From the "sharp two-edged sword" (Revelation 1:16) coming out of the mouth of the "One like the Son of Man" (Revelation 1:13), until "Death and Hades" (Revelation 20:14) are cast in the lake of fire, the book exudes imagery and symbolism. What is literal, and what is symbolic, and how does one tell the difference?

Fortunately, Revelation doesn't exist in a vacuum. It is only one of the sixty-six books that can help differentiate between the symbolic and the real in Revelation.

The Old Testament and, particularly, the New teach the existence of a heavenly sanctuary. In Exodus 25:8, 9, the Lord gave Moses instruction for building the earthly tabernacle. "Let them make Me a sanctuary, that I may dwell among them. . . . According to all that I show you, that is, the *pattern* of the tabernacle and the *pattern* of all its furnishing, just so you shall make it."[4]

"Pattern" is translated from the Hebrew *tabnit*, which is linked to the verb *bnh*, "to build." In the Hebrew Bible, *bnh* (in

70

various conjugations) refers to the building of cities, walls, houses, ramparts, temples, and a fortress.[5] In Amos 9:6, the verb is used to say that the Lord built in heaven His "roof-chamber."[6]

Besides "pattern," *tabnit* itself is translated "figure," "construction," "image," or "replica," and is used often in relation to real objects. The children of Israel wanted to build an altar so that future generations could say, "Here is the replica [*tabnit*] of the altar of the Lord which our fathers made" (Joshua 22:28). Moses warned the children of Israel not to make for themselves "a carved image in the form [*tabnit*] of any figure: the likeness [*tabnit*] of male or female" (Deuteronomy 4:16).

When the Lord showed Moses a *tabnit* in Exodus 28, did Moses see only a blueprint, or did he see a *tabnit* of a real sanctuary in heaven? Though the word *tabnit* itself could imply something physical, it doesn't have to. "To be sure," writes Niels-Eric Andreason, "the texts themselves . . . do not require the existence of a heavenly sanctuary serving as a model. A divinely revealed plan for the earthly sanctuary would satisfy the expression *tabnit*. Nevertheless, the majority of commentators support the existence of a heavenly sanctuary in these verses. . . ." 7, 8, 9.

Fortunately, other Old Testament verses hint at a literal temple in heaven. "Hear, all you peoples! Listen, O earth, and all that is in it! Let the Lord God be a witness against you, the Lord from His holy temple. For behold, the Lord is coming out of His place; He will come down and tread on the high places of the earth" (Micah 1:2, 3).

"The Lord is in His holy temple, the Lord's throne is in heaven" (Psalm 11:4).

Psalm 68:34, 35 reads: "Proclaim the power of God, whose majesty is over Israel, whose power is in the skies. You are awesome, O god, in your sanctuary" (NIV).

Evidence of the heavenly temple appears in Daniel 8:14— "He said to me, For two thousand three hundred days; then the sanctuary shall be cleansed." In isolation, it would be hard to know what sanctuary Daniel means, but in context it becomes obvious. The cleansing of this sanctuary happens at the end of the vision of chapter 8, which includes a ram (Media-Persia), a he-goat (Greece), and a little horn (pagan and papal Rome). Thus, the chronology of verse 14—coming *after* a phase of papal Rome—places the cleansing of the sanctuary centuries after the earthly sanctuary was destroyed.[10] The only option would be that this verse is speaking of the sanctuary in heaven being cleansed.[11]

Also, the cleansing of the sanctuary in verse 14 parallels the heavenly judgment depicted in Daniel 7. Because they are the same events,[12] and because Daniel 7 is clearly a heavenly event,[13] then the cleansing of the sanctuary in Daniel 8 must be in heaven as well.

The most powerful evidence for a heavenly sanctuary, however, is found in the book of Hebrews.

"Now this is the main point of the things we are saying: We have such a High Priest, who is seated at the right hand of the throne of the Majesty in the heavens, a Minister of *the true tabernacle* which the Lord erected, not man" (Hebrews 8:1, 2, emphasis supplied).

The author, after talking about the earthly sanctuary, then says that it was "the copy and shadow of the heavenly things" (verse 5).

Again, after talking about the earthly, temporal sanctuary service, the author writes that "Christ came as High Priest of the good things to come, with *the greater and more perfect tabernacle not made with hands*, that is, not of this creation. Not with the blood of goats and calves, but with His own blood He entered the Most Holy Place once for all, having obtained eternal redemption" (Hebrews 9:11, 12).

Not only is the heavenly sanctuary "the greater and more perfect" tabernacle, but interestingly enough, it, too, needs to be cleansed: "It was necessary that the copies of the things in the heavens should be purified with these [the blood of animal sacrifices], but the heavenly things themselves with better sacrifices than these" (verse 23). Obviously, if the heavenly things need to be cleansed, they must exist.

No wonder Hebrews scholar William Johnsson wrote that the book of Hebrews, "on the face of it, presents the strongest statements in the Bible in support of an actual heavenly sanctuary and ministry."[14]

Nevertheless, some scholars claim that the author of Hebrews had been heavily influenced by Plato's "ideas and forms" and therefore was not talking about a physical structure in heaven. It's all Platonic metaphor.

Plato (c. 429–347 B.C.) believed that the world we live in and experience with our senses, the phenomenal sphere, isn't the real world, but a shadow, a copy of the essence of reality. This phenomenal world is, he wrote, "human, mortal, multiform, unintelligible, dissolvable and never self-consistent."[15] He compared the human understanding of the world to people chained from childhood in a cave and forced to look only at the innermost wall. Behind them was a fire, and whatever passed between them and the fire would cast shadows upon the wall before them. For these people, Plato said, the only reality was the shadows. "Would they not assume," he wrote in the *Republic*, "that the shadows they saw were the real thing?"[16]

In contrast to the shadows on a cave wall, Plato believed that true reality existed in "ideas or forms," a transcendent existence of "changeless, eternal, and nonmaterial essences or patterns of which the actual visible objects we see are only poor copies."[17] A triangle, for example, is only a copy of the nonmaterial, transcendent perfect triangle, and it becomes a triangle only as it partakes of the "form" of a triangle. Something is beautiful only as it shares in the absolute "form" or "idea" of beauty. "I am assuming the existence," Plato wrote, "of absolute Beauty and Goodness and Magnitude. . . . It seems to me that whatever else is beautiful apart from absolute Beauty is beautiful because it partakes of that absolute beauty, and for no other reason."[18]

These Platonic concepts, filtered and modified by the great Jewish Hellenist Philo of Judea (c. 20 B.C.–A.D. 50), are supposedly the philosophical basis for the book Hebrews, according to some scholars. Thus, for these scholars, when Hebrews talks about the "true tabernacle" (Hebrews 8:2) or the "greater and more perfect tabernacle" (Hebrews 9:11), in contrast to the mere "shadow" (Hebrew 10:1) or "copies" (Hebrews 9:24) on earth, the author was echoing these Platonic concepts via Philo. For this reason, many commentators believe references in Hebrews to a heavenly sanctuary are only metaphorical, and that no real sanctuary exists in heaven. Even Adventists who deny the reality of the heavenly sanctuary do so from this influence.

No doubt, the Bible writers were influenced by their own environment, even though the Bible was "given by inspiration of God" (2 Timothy 3:16). But how extensive was that influence? It's one thing for Paul, given the world he inhabited, to send the slave Onesimus back to Philemon (though it would be hard to imagine him sending an escaped slave back to a southern plantation), but it's another thing to believe that a central theme of Hebrews was rooted in a Greek philosopher who taught, among other things, that in an ideal society, "children should be held in common, and no parent should know its child, or child its parent,"[19] or that at death some souls hover "about tombs and graveyards."[20]

But even more conclusively, a deeper look at Hebrews proves that though the writer may have borrowed some Platonic language, Hebrews is definitely not influenced by Platonic ideas. Hebrews talks about Jesus entering into a place ("passed through the heavens" [4:14], "behind the veil" [6:19], "sat down at the right hand of God" [10:12]), a concept totally foreign to Plato's "ideas and forms," which are not spatial and can't be physically entered. "Plato's Ideal world," wrote R. Williamson, "is not a heaven that could be entered even by Jesus; it can be penetrated only by the intellect."[21]

The central idea of Hebrews is that Jesus became our High Priest and entered into heaven *at a certain time*. "The Holy Spirit indicating this, that the way into the Holiest of All was not yet made manifest while the first tabernacle was still standing. . . . Not with the blood of goats and calves, but with His own blood He entered the Most Holy Place once for all" (Hebrews 9:8, 12). This concept contradicts the eternal timelessness of Plato's "ideas and forms" and Philo's understanding of them.

"With these ideas," writes William Johnsson, "the sanctuary language of Hebrews diverges sharply from the Philonic model. We can no longer hold to an eternal, unchanged and unchanging heavenly order, far removed from and untouched by events on earth."[22]

Hebrews says that the "copies of the things in the heavens should be purified" (Hebrews 9:23), a position radically contradictory to Plato's "ideas and forms," which are perfect and absolute.

Hebrews is Christian theology, not Greek metaphysics. If anything, Hebrews reflects Jewish thought all through history, which taught that a sanctuary in heaven existed.

"The [earthly] sanctuary corresponds with that of the heavenly sanctuary," says one ancient source, "and the ark with that of the heavenly throne."[23]

The Babylonian Talmud talks about "the heavenly and earthly Temples,"[24] and the Jerusalem Talmud says that "the earthly Holy of Holies is just under the heavenly holy of holies."[25]

Another ancient source says that "there is no difference of opinion that the sanctuary below is the counterpart of the sanctuary above."[26]

According to the Talmud, the Jews believed that seven things existed prior to the creation of the world, and among them was the heavenly temple.[27]

Says another source: "And thereupon the angel opened to me the gates of heaven, and I saw a holy temple, and upon a throne of glory the Most High."[28]

The Jews believed not only that there was a sanctuary in heaven, but that a ministry was performed there as well. "Why," asks the Talmud, "is the high priest clothed in white on the Day of Atonement?" And it answers: "Because the service in the terrestrial Temple must equal that in the Heavenly Temple."[29] According to the *Jewish Encyclopedia*, "The rabbis speak of Michael (Metatron) as the captain of the heavenly host, as the high priest that offers sacrifice in the upper temple."[30] The idea of Michael as the high priest became so prevalent among the Jews that they began praying directly to him, a practice the rabbis forbade. The Jews eventually saw Michael, as high priest, "making atonement for his people."[31]

Whatever the noncanonical thought, the canonical Scriptures themselves are clear that a literal sanctuary in heaven exists. Because Hebrews teaches that after His sacrifice, Jesus entered into a ministry in the heavenly sanctuary and because Revelation is filled with images of Jesus as High Priest and of the sanctuary—whatever else is symbolic, the visions of Christ and the heavenly sanctuary must be visions of real things depicting spiritual truths. When, for instance, Revelation talks about a Lamb in heaven, it's using a symbol to depict a spiritual truth, yet that symbol stands for a reality, in this case, Jesus.

"One cannot demythologize," writes Dick Davidson, "the reality of the heavenly sanctuary, dismissing it as imagery within the symbolic world of apocalyptic literature. The OT [Old Testament] control passages, which clearly form the backdrop to the sanctuary descriptions of Revelation, in all their manifold witness of different writers using different genres (including apocalyptic), unitedly uphold the objective reality of the heavenly sanctuary."[32]

But is there an altar in the heavenly sanctuary upon which an angel burns incense mingled with the prayers of the saints, as depicted in Revelation? Many Adventists would insist yes, and would claim that any departure from that belief is apostasy. For them, a one-to-one correspondence between heaven and earth is the only safe way to understand the heavenly sanctuary, and to remove, move, or symbolize even a curtain rod would be to tamper with eternal truths.

Extreme literalism, however, runs into problems. When David encouraged Solomon to build the temple, the king gave him details for the court, the chambers around it, the vessels of service, the weight of the candlesticks, everything. " 'All this,' said David, 'the Lord made me understand in writing, by His hand upon me, all the works of these *plans*' " (1 Chronicles 28:19, emphasis supplied).

The word for "plans" is *tabnit*. Yet the divinely revealed *tabnit* of Solomon's temple didn't duplicate the divinely revealed *tabnit* of the wilderness temple. Solomon's temple varied in numerous ways: it had two courts, the wilderness temple had one; Solomon's temple had ten lampstands, the wilderness temple had one; Solomon's temple had ten tables of shewbread, the wilderness temple had one; Solomon's temple had ten lavers, the wilderness temple had one, and on and on. If the earthly temple followed an exact one-to-one correspondence with the heavenly, which one—the wilderness sanctuary or Solomon's temple—was closer to the original?

"If both the wilderness tabernacle and the Jerusalem Temple were constructed according to the heavenly pattern," asks Roy Adams, "how can 'pattern' be understood in a strictly literal sense when in so many details the two structures exhibited such striking dissimilarities? And the situation becomes even more complex when we take into account the further variations and developments indicated in Ezekiel's ideal Temple (Ezekiel 40:1–43:27). . . . At the very least such differences ought to steer us away from dogmatizing about the appearance of the heavenly sanctuary based on our knowledge of the earthly."[33]

Also, a crucial aspect of the earthly sanctuary service, if not its foundation, was the altar of burnt offering upon which the animals were slain. Is there an altar of burnt offering in heaven? If so, what would be its purpose, now that "once at the end of the ages, He [Christ] has appeared to put away sin by the sacrifice of Himself" (Hebrews 9:26)?

Of course, the Bible never says that an altar for sacrifice exists in heaven, so the question could be moot. But that's the point. The Bible doesn't place an altar of burnt offering in heaven, because its function was fulfilled on earth, at the cross. But if this crucial part of the sanctuary service doesn't exist in the heavenly structure, can other parts of the sanctuary service be missing from the heavenly structure as well? Or better phrased, can other parts of the heavenly sanctuary be "spiritualized" too?

Yes, and the way the cross spiritualized the altar of burnt offering shows the way other aspects of the sanctuary can be spiritualized without denying their ultimate, and even greater, reality.[34]

The altar of burnt offering in the wilderness tabernacle was a foursquare wooden structure (see Exodus 27:1) covered with copper plates (see Exodus 27:1, 2, 8; Numbers 16:37, 38). Wooden horns overlaid with copper extended from its four corners (see Exodus 27:2). Besides the altar itself, various utensils for sacrifices—knives, fleshhooks, basins, rakes, shovels, fire pans, etc.— were part of the altar service, not including the wood for burning as well as the most important element: the slain animals, which produced flesh, fat, and blood.

Yet however real, tangible, and physical the altar and its services were—they existed only as a type, a symbol, a shadow of Christ's death, the greater and more perfect reality. Every sacrifice, every speck of the endless streams of blood spilled for centuries, either in the wilderness or the Jerusalem cultus, merely prefigured the greater spiritual reality of Calvary. These "shadows," in and of themselves, couldn't save anyone, because "it is not possible that the blood of bulls and goats could take away sins" (Hebrews 10:4). Only by the blood of Jesus can a person have "forgiveness of sins, according to the riches of His grace" (Ephesians 1:7).

The death of Jesus on the cross, not that of a goat or ten thousand goats on the altar, brings salvation. Thus, though the physical reality of Christ on the cross was just as real as the physical reality of the typical sacrifices, its spiritual reality vastly overshadows anything that happened on the earthly altar. And, too, long after the altar of burnt offerings has vanished, the physical reality of the cross will remain, forever etched in the scars on the hands of Him who was wounded in the house of His friends (see Zechariah 13:6).[35] In every way, the cross was greater, more perfect, and more enduring than the sacrifices on the altar of burnt offerings.

Calvary was the one aspect of the plan of salvation, as taught in the sanctuary, that remained distinctly earthly. The rest of the sanctuary ministration takes place in heaven, with Jesus as High Priest. Once the shift to heaven occurs, why deny its physical reality? Are the heavenly realities any less real than Calvary?

"The difference between the earthly and the heavenly sanctuary," writes Dick Davidson, "is not that the heavenly is less literal, less real, as our western overdose of Greek thought might lead us unsuspectingly to suppose."[36] Indeed, what little is known about the heavenly sanctuary[37] indicates that "the greater and more perfect tabernacle" (Hebrews 9:11) and whatever is in it would be more real than the earthly, which was merely "an example and shadow" (Hebrews 8:5) and a "figure of the true" (Hebrews 9:24).

THE ALTAR OF INCENSE

In the Most Holy Place of the earthly tabernacle were two gold cherubim. "And you shall make two cherubim of gold; of hammered work you shall make them at the two ends of the mercy seat. . . . And they shall face one another; the faces of the cherubim shall be toward the mercy seat" (Exodus 25:18, 20). Cherubim were woven on the curtain inside the sanctuary, as well (see Exodus 26:31).

These inanimate cherubim in the earthly sanctuary obviously symbolized the "thousand thousands [who] ministered to Him; Ten thousand times ten thousand [that] stood before him" (Daniel 7:10) in the heavenly sanctuary. All through Revelation, angelic beings are linked with the heavenly sanctuary: "And another angel came out of the temple" (Revelation 14:15). "And another angel came out from the altar" (Revelation 14:18). "After these things I looked, and behold, the temple of the tabernacle of the testimony in heaven was opened. And out of the temple came the seven angels having the seven plagues" (Revelation 15:5, 6). "Then I looked, and I heard the voice of many angels around the throne, the living creatures, and the elders; and the number of them was ten thousand times ten thousand, and thousands of thousands" (Revelation 5:11).

What is more real, two gold statues and a few figures woven on curtains, or hundreds of thousands of angels? These heavenly beings are a reality far greater than their earthly symbols, just as the cross represented a reality far greater than the altar that symbolized it. No wonder the author of Hebrews, in contrasting the earthly sanctuary to the heavenly, called the heavenly the "greater and more perfect" reality (Hebrews 9:11) and the earthly merely a "copy and a shadow" (Hebrews 8:5).

On one end of the sanctuary service is the cross; on the other, the angelic host. If the cross and the angels represent things more real than their symbols, why should the rest of the heavenly sanctuary be any less real than the symbols used to represent them?[38] Why spiritualize in Revelation what other scriptures make literal?

Is there, then, an altar in the heavenly sanctuary where an angel offers incense? For what reason? Incense can't make our prayers acceptable to God, any more than the blood of bulls and cows can justify us. Although the Bible doesn't give enough information to know exactly what does exist in the heavenly sanctuary, whatever does is a "greater and more perfect" reality than the altar on earth, just as the altar of burnt offerings and the two gold cherubim symbolized things more real than themselves. The dogmatic insistence that each piece of furniture in the earthly must exist in the heavenly, instead of strengthening the argument for the reality of the celestial sanctuary, weakens it—because what's up there is more real than just a copper-plated wooden box with four horns attached to its corners, a golden candlestick, or a table with two piles of bread. A "greater and more perfect tabernacle," whatever that means, isn't a hollow shell.

Also, if "it is not possible that the blood of bulls and goats could take away sins" (Hebrews 10:4), what was the purpose of the earthly temple? If none of those endless sacrifices could atone for transgression, why did the Lord institute the slaughter of millions of helpless, innocent creatures? Wasn't it to teach the world about salvation, from the death of the spotless "lamb of God" to the final separation of sin from sinners? As "a shadow of the good things to come" (Hebrews 10:1), wasn't the sanctuary's purpose instructive? Paul said that the gospel had been preached to ancient Israel (see Hebrews 4:2), and the sanctuary service was one of the clearest ways that the Lord did it.[39]

Now, just as the earthly sanctuary taught terrestrial beings about salvation, couldn't the heavenly teach celestial inhabitants about it as well? Heavenly intelligences are, beyond question, interested in the plan of salvation, and just as the earthly instructed us, might not the "greater" instruct them?[40]

Revelation shows celestial beings watching—and responding to—God's activity in the heavenly sanctuary. When Jesus receives the scroll with the seven seals, the angels in the sanctuary exclaim: "Worthy is the Lamb who was slain to receive power and riches and wisdom, and strength and honor and glory and blessing!" (Revelation 5:12). After the seals are unloosed, those angels praise Him again: "Amen! Blessing and glory and wisdom, thanksgiving and honor and power and might, be to our God forever and ever. Amen" (Revelation 7:12). After the angels leave the heavenly temple with the seven plagues ("and out of the temple came the seven angels having the seven plagues" [Revelation 15:6]), which they start pouring out upon the earth, an angel from the sanctuary exclaims, "Even so, Lord God Almighty, true and righteous are Your judgments!" (Revelation 16:7). These angels in the sanctuary have been watching what the Lord is doing in heaven and, obviously, as the bigger picture unfolds, they rejoice in the deeds and power of God.

Of course, more important than the literalness of the heavenly sanctuary are its spiritual truths. Function supersedes form, and Revelation's third sanctuary scene, with its emphasis on the altar of incense, indicates the continual intercession of Christ as our High Priest. Though Jesus isn't mentioned, "the scene portrayed may be understood as symbolic of the ministration of Christ for His people. . . . Christ, as intercessor, mingles His merits with the prayers of the saints, which are thereby made acceptable with God."[41]

Just as priests ministered the incense on behalf of God's people, Christ's righteousness alone—not an altar burning with incense—makes our prayers acceptable to the Lord. The issue is not whether there is real incense in the heavenly sanctuary; the issue is the work of Christ as our intercessor: "If anyone sins, we have an Advocate with the Father, Jesus Christ the righteous" (1 John 2:1). "Therefore He is also able to save to the uttermost those who come to God through Him, since He ever lives to make intercession for them" (Hebrews 7:25).

What this third sanctuary scene implies, with all the symbolism taken into consideration, is that Christ's work for us continues. The same loving Saviour, who died on the cross for us, is now working for us in heaven. The sanctuary teaches that the righteousness of Christ, wrought by His perfect life and atoning death, doesn't stop at the cross. That righteousness—His righteousness—is carried over into His work on our behalf in heaven, and it is the only thing that makes even our prayers, much less ourselves, acceptable to the Father.

What else, then, do we need?

BETWEEN THE LAMB AND THE LION

1. "The subject of the sanctuary was the key which unlocked the mystery of the disappointment of 1844. It opened to view a complete system of truth, connected and harmonious, showing that God's hand had directed the great advent movement and revealing present duty as it brought to light the position and work of His people" (*The Great Controversy*, 423).

2. P. Gerard Damsteegt, "Among Sabbatarian Adventists," in *Doctrine of the Sanctuary: A Historical Survey*, 43, Frank Holbrook, ed. (Silver Spring, Md.: General Conference of Seventh-day Adventists, 1989), 43.

3. "The enemy will bring in false theories, such as the doctrine that there is no sanctuary. This is one of the points on which there will be a departing from the faith" (*Evangelism*, 224).

4. See also 1 Chronicles 28:19.

5. See Brown, Driver, and Briggs, *Hebrew and English Lexicon of the Old Testament*.

6. This word has also been translated "stairs" or "layers." "Roof chamber" comes from Brown, Driver, and Briggs, under the root *bnh*.

7. Niels-Eric Andreason, "The Heavenly Sanctuary in the Old Testament," in *The Sanctuary and the Atonement*, Richard Lesher and Arnold Wallenkamp, eds., 69. For a list of commentators who do see a literal sanctuary in those verses, see above article, footnote 21.

8. "The command was communicated to Moses while in the mount with God, 'Let them make me a sanctuary that I may dwell among them;' and full directions were given for the construction of the tabernacle. . . . God presented before Moses in the mount a view of the heavenly sanctuary, and commanded him to make all things according to the pattern shown him" (*Patriarchs and Prophets*, 343).

9. For a more detailed study of *tabnit*, see Dick Davidson, *Typology in Scripture* (Berrien Springs, Mich.: Andrews University Press, 1981), 367, 388.

10. Gerhard Hasel, "The Little Horn, the Heavenly Sanctuary and the Time of the End: A Study of Daniel 8:9-14," in *Symposium on Daniel*, Frank Holbrook, ed. (Washington, D.C.: General Conference of Seventh-day Adventists, 1986), 378-426.

11. "The sanctuary in heaven, in which Jesus ministers in our behalf, is the great original, of which the sanctuary built by Moses was a copy. . . . The matchless splendor of the earthly tabernacle reflected to human vision the glories of that heavenly temple where Christ our forerunner ministers for us before the throne of God. The abiding place of the King of kings, where thousand thousands minister unto Him,

and ten thousand times ten thousand stand before Him (Daniel 7:10); that temple, filled with the glory of the eternal throne, where seraphim, its shining guardians, veil their faces in adoration, could find, in the most magnificent structure reared by humans, but a faint reflection of its vastness and glory" (*The Great Controversy*, 414).

"Thus those who were studying the subject found indisputable proof of the existence of a sanctuary in heaven. Moses made the earthly sanctuary after a pattern which was shown him. Paul teaches that pattern was the true sanctuary which is in heaven. And John testifies that he saw it in heaven" (ibid., 415).

12. William H. Shea, "Unity of Daniel," in *Symposium on Daniel,* 165-220.

13. It has thrones being put in place, the Ancient of Days sitting, fiery streams coming out from before him, ten thousand times ten thousand beings ministering to Him, the Son of Man coming with clouds of heaven to the Ancient of Days, books being opened, and a judgment commencing. Clearly, this is a heavenly event.

14. William Johnsson, "The Heavenly Sanctuary—Figurative or Real?" in *Issues in the Book of Hebrews,* Frank Holbrook, ed. (Washington, D.C.: General Conference of Seventh-day Adventists, 1989), 40.

15. Plato, *Phaedo*, 80b (New York: Penguin Books, 1969), 132.

16. Plato, *The Republic* (New York: Penguin Books, 1987), 317.

17. Samuel Enoch Strumph, *From Socrates to Sartre* (New York: McGraw-Hill, 1982), 56.

18. Plato, *Phaedo*, 158, 159.

19. Plato, *Republic*, 237.

20. Plato, *Phaedo*, 133.

21. R. Williamson, "Platonism and Hebrews," *Scottish Journal of Theology* 16 (1963), 419.

22. Johnsson, "The Heavenly Sanctuary—Figurative or Real?" 45.

23. Midrash Rabbah on Numbers, chapter 4., sec. 13., Soncino edition, 1:110, 111.

24. Sanhedrin 99b.

25. Berakoth, chap. 4., Mishnah 5.

26. Midrash on Psalms. Psalm 30. sec. 1.

27. Pesahim 54a.

28. Testament of Levi 5:1.

29. *The Jewish Encyclopedia*, 11:616.

30. *The Jewish Encyclopedia*, 1:596.

31. Ibid., 8:537.

32. Davidson, "Sanctuary Typology," in *Symposium on Revelation*, 103, 104.

33. Roy Adams, *The Sanctuary* (Hagerstown, Md.: Review and Herald, 1993), 54.

34. "Two dangers must be avoided. We can concentrate solely on the 'heavenly geography' and lose the spiritual messages that are communicated. But we can also spiritualize away the spatiotemporal reality and thereby lose both the literal substance and spiritual truth." Davidson, "Sanctuary Typology," 106.

35. "One reminder alone remains: Our Redeemer will ever bear the marks of His crucifixion. Upon His wounded head, upon His side, His hands and feet, are the only traces of the cruel work that sin has wrought" *(The Great Controversy*, 674. See also the *SDA Bible Commentary*, 7:955).

36. Davidson, "Sanctuary Typology," 104.

37. "While we may affirm the *reality* of the heavenly sanctuary in the book of Hebrews, we have comparatively little hard data about its appearance" (Johnsson, "The Heavenly Sanctuary—Figurative or Real?" 51).

38. "As in vision the apostle John was granted a view of the temple of God in heaven, he beheld there 'seven lamps of fire burning before the throne.' Revelation 4:5. He saw an angel 'having a golden censer; and there was given unto him much incense, that he should offer it with the prayers of all saints upon the golden altar which was before the throne.' Revelation 8:3. Here the prophet was permitted to behold the first apartment of the sanctuary in heaven; and he saw there the 'seven lamps of fire' and 'the golden altar,' represented by the golden candlestick and the altar of incense in the sanctuary on earth. Again, the 'temple of God was opened' (Revelation 11:19), and he looked within the inner veil, upon the holy of holies. Here he beheld 'the ark of His testament,' represented by the sacred chest constructed by Moses to contain the law of God" *(The Great Controversy*, 414, 415).

39. "All who did service in connection with the sanctuary were being educated constantly in regard to the intervention of Christ in behalf of the human race. This service was designed to create in every heart a love for the law of God, which is the law of His kingdom. The sacrificial offering was to be an object lesson of the love of God revealed in Christ" *(Selected Messages*, 1:233).

40. See *False Balances*, 53-133.

41. *SDA Bible Commentary*, 7:787.

Chapter
Eight
THE HOUR OF HIS JUDGMENT

A lthough the first three heavenly-sanctuary scenes in Revelation deal with the first apartment, the fourth goes directly to the second apartment—the Most Holy Place: "Then the temple of God was opened in heaven, and the ark of His covenant was seen in His temple. And there were lightnings, noises, thunderings, an earthquake, and great hail" (Revelation 11:19).[1]

"The ark of His covenant" (Revelation 11:19)—also called the "ark of the Testimony" (Exodus 25:22), the "ark of the covenant of the Lord" (Numbers 10:33), and the "ark of the covenant of God" (Judges 20:27)—was the gold-covered wooden chest that held Aaron's rod, a pot of manna, and the two tablets upon which God had written the Ten Commandments. Above the ark rested the mercy seat, and both ark and mercy seat sat in the Most Holy Place, where once a year the high priest ministered on the Day of Atonement, the time of judgment for God's people.

No wonder, then, that the Most Holy Place first appears in the book of Revelation in the context of judgment. In the verses just before John sees the ark of the covenant in the temple in heaven, the twenty-four elders in heaven are praising God, saying, " 'We give You thanks, O Lord God Almighty . . . because You have taken Your great power and reigned. The nations were angry, and Your wrath has come, and the time of the dead, that they should be judged, and that You should reward Your servants the prophets and the saints, and those who fear Your name, small and great, and should destroy those who destroy the earth' " (Revelation 11:17, 18).

It's time to judge the dead, and among them are God's "servants the prophets and the saints." This judgment is obviously positive; it is judgment for, even on behalf of, these people, because as a result they receive their reward. Thus, the next verse reveals the Most Holy Place, where in the earthly sanctuary, judgment also took place—judgment on behalf of God's faithful people. With the exception of the inauguration of the earthly sanctuary, the High Priest entered the second apartment only for judgment. For this reason, after progressing from the Holy to the Most Holy Place, Revelation heralds the judgment hour message: " 'Fear God and give glory to Him, for the hour of His judgment has come' " (Revelation 14:7).

Except for Revelation 6:10, which calls for a judgment that has not yet happened, the Apocalypse is devoid of judgment language until Revelation 11:18, which immediately leads into the Most Holy Place in the next verse. Only *after* this second-apartment scene do the common words for judgment (*krisis, krima, krino*) appear: "For Your judgments have been manifested" (15:4). "He has judged the great harlot" (19:2). "In righteousness He judges and makes war" (19:11). "They were judged, every one according to his works" (20:13). Judgment doesn't happen until the transition from the first to the second apartment occurs, and the second apartment doesn't come into view until the last half of the book.[2]

This transition is one of the most important of all the heavenly-sanctuary introduction scenes, because the judgment it represents is the pivotal event that precedes the consummation of salvation: the second coming of Jesus.[3]

The move to the Most Holy Place and the vision of the "ark of His covenant" automatically introduces the Ten Commandments that were placed inside the ark. Not surprisingly, then, after the view of the Most Holy Place in heaven, two verses in Revelation mention obedience to the Ten Commandments: the dragon seeks to make war with "the remnant of her seed, which keep the commandments of God" (Revelation 12:17, KJV). "Here is the patience of the saints: here are they that keep the commandments of God, and the faith of Jesus" (Revelation 14:12,

KJV). Revelation unites the Most Holy Place in the heavenly sanctuary with judgment and the commandments of God.[4]

In Revelation 14, the first angel announces that God's judgment has come. And before the chapter ends, another angel comes "out of the temple" with a sickle in order "to reap, for the harvest of the earth is ripe" (Revelation 14:15). Christ is coming to receive His people, but before He does so, He judges them in a process by which He sifts the wheat from the chaff. Judgment is linked to the second coming; actually, judgment is the prerequisite for His coming.

"The Lord will judge His people" (Hebrews 10:30).

"Be patient. Establish your hearts, for the coming of the Lord is at hand. Do not grumble against one another, brethren, lest you be condemned. Behold, the Judge is standing at the door!" (James 5:8, 9).

"Let both grow together until the harvest, and at the time of harvest I will say to the reapers, 'First gather together the tares and bind them in bundles to burn them, but gather the wheat into my barn' " (Matthew 13:30).

"When the king came in to see the guests, he saw a man there who did not have on a wedding garment. So he said to him, 'Friend, how did you come in here without a wedding garment?' And he was speechless. Then the king said to the servants, 'Bind him hand and foot, take him away, and cast him into outer darkness' " (Matthew 22:11-13).

"He will thoroughly purge His threshing floor, and gather the wheat into His barn; but the chaff He will burn with unquenchable fire" (Luke 3:17).

"And while they went to buy, the bridegroom came, and those who were ready went in with him to the wedding; and the door was shut. Afterward the other virgins came also, saying, 'Lord, Lord, open to us!' But he answered and said, 'Assuredly, I say to you, I do not know you.' Watch therefore, for you know neither the day nor the hour in which the Son of Man is coming" (Matthew 25:10-13).

Prior to the second coming, there is a judgment of God's professed people in which the Lord will separate the faithful from the unfaithful. "The pre-Advent judgment," writes Edward

Heppenstall, "is the prelude to the coming of Christ and the establishment of His kingdom. The apostle John, in Revelation 14:6-20, speaks of the coming of Christ as dependent upon a judgment that makes it possible for Him to 'render to every man according to his deeds' (Romans 2:6, [KJV]). This judgment is portrayed under the figures of the harvest of wheat, the righteous—and the harvest of the grapes, the unrepentant."[5]

Of course, no aspect of Adventism has come under more attack than the pre-advent judgment, particularly because it supposedly nullifies the cross.[6]

No doubt, the investigative judgment has been taught in an anti-gospel manner, which helps explain the antipathy toward it; but it's a big lie that the doctrine itself is anti-gospel. On the contrary, far from negating the cross, the pre-advent judgment brings what Christ accomplished at Calvary to its climax.

Because the Ten Commandments are linked to the judgment, the tendency has been to emphasize law more than grace, even though the investigative judgment is about almost nothing but grace. The emphasis in Revelation 11:19 is on *the ark* that contains the law, not the law itself. On the Levitical Day of Atonement, the earthly type of the heavenly judgment, almost everything that happened revolved around blood, not law.

> He shall take some of the *blood* of the bull and sprinkle it with his finger on the mercy seat on the east side; and before the mercy seat he shall sprinkle some of the *blood* with his finger seven times. Then he shall kill the goat of the sin offering, which is for the people, bring its *blood* inside the veil, do with that *blood* as he did with the *blood* of the bull, and sprinkle it on the mercy seat and before the mercy seat. . . . And he shall go out to the altar that is before the Lord, and make atonement for it, and shall take some of the *blood* of the bull and some of the *blood* of the goat, and put it on the horns of the altar all around. Then he shall sprinkle some of the *blood* on it with his finger seven times, cleanse it, and sanctify it from the uncleanness of the children of Israel (Leviticus 16:14, 15, 18, 19, emphasis supplied).

With the exception of the scapegoat—a symbol of Satan, not Christ[7]—blood is the key element on the Day of Atonement. "For the life of the flesh is in the blood, and I have given it to you upon the altar to make atonement for your souls; for it is the blood that makes atonement for the soul" (Leviticus 17:11). Blood, not the law, atoned for sin, and every drop symbolized the only blood that truly makes atonement, the blood of Christ.[8] "You were not redeemed with corruptible things, like silver or gold, from your aimless conduct received by tradition from your fathers, but with the precious blood of Christ, as of a lamb without blemish and without spot" (1 Peter 1:18, 19).

Just as blood was the only thing that got the penitent Israelite through the earthly Day of Atonement, so it is blood, Christ's blood, that gets the penitent today through the heavenly Day of Atonement. In the daily ministry, Christ as Intercessor presents His own perfect life in place of the repentant sinner's imperfect one; in the yearly service, He does the same thing. Whenever the name of one of His true followers appears for judgment,[9] Christ pleads His blood,[10] His righteousness, in that person's stead.

"The pre-Advent judgment," writes Norman Gulley, "is Christ-centered and not man-centered. It is not so much what individuals have or have not done per se that is decisive. Rather it is whether they have accepted or rejected what Christ has done for them when He was judged in their place at the cross (John 12:31)."[11]

Christ's yearly ministry is better news than His daily, because in the yearly His blood covers sinners *once and for all.* Under the daily ministration, a sinner can be covered—only to eventually turn away and be lost. Once, however, Christ gets us through the judgment by virtue of His blood, His perfection, His robe of righteousness (see Matthew 22:1-13)—we are "once saved always saved," and never in danger of falling away. When the names of the truly penitent come up in the judgment, they are forever sealed, eternally secure in Christ. "He who is righteous, let him be righteous still; he who is holy, let him be holy still" (Revelation 22:11), and the only way we can be deemed "holy" and "righteous" in the sight of God—no matter how obedient, faithful, and sanctified we become by His indwelling Holy Spirit—is by the imputed righteousness of Christ, the righteousness that Christ once and for all pleads on our behalf in the pre-advent judgment.

When the High Priest entered the second apartment in the earthly sanctuary, he twice sprinkled blood "on the mercy seat and before the mercy seat" (Leviticus 16:15).

"Mercy seat" is an imaginative translation of the difficult Hebrew word *kapporet*, from the root *kpr*. The origins of *kpr* are debated, and scholars link it with "wash away" or "rub off," but it has commonly been translated "to make propitiation," "to pacify," "to cover," "to atone." It's often translated as atonement.[12] "For the life of the flesh is in the blood, and I have given it to you upon the altar to make atonement [from *kpr*] for your souls; for it is the blood that makes atonement for the soul" (Leviticus 17:11). "And it came to pass on the next day that Moses said to the people, 'You have sinned a great sin. So now I will go up to the Lord; perhaps I can make atonement [from *kpr*] for your sin' " (Exodus 32:30, KJV).

The verb is also used for "ransom." In ancient Israel, if a man owned an ox known to be violent and it killed a person, the owner either had to pay with his life or make financial restitution: "If there be laid on him a sum of money, then he shall give for the ransom [from *kpr*] of his life whatsoever is laid upon him" (Exodus 21:30, KJV).

Thus, blood is used to spare the guilty. Whatever *kpr* may mean exactly, it clearly covers and expiates transgression.

The *kapporet*, or "mercy seat," was central to the Day of Atonement. The blood of an innocent animal was accepted on behalf of the sinner, and that blood was sprinkled upon and before the *kapporet*, which itself implied atonement and covering. The *kapporet* was not lifted or removed on the Day of Atonement. It covered the law, which never came into view, because this was the Day of *Atonement*, and the law cannot atone for anything or anyone. It is the blood that atoned.

It's too late for our obedience to the law to atone for our sins. No one has ever kept the law, or ever will keep it, well enough to be saved by it. Only the righteousness of Christ—symbolized by the blood and by the *kapporet*—gets us through the judgment.

Thus, in the pre-advent judgment, typified by the Yom Kippur ritual, it's what Christ has done as our atonement that covers us. It's not our obedience to the law—however important that may be—that allows us to stand perfect, holy, and righteous in the sight of God during judgment. Only the righteousness that Christ imputes (credits) to us—forensic righteousness—can seal us on the Day of Atonement.

There are those who reject forensic righteousness. They fear that it is an excuse to sin. Those who have that attitude, however, have never experienced justification by faith personally, for those who have experienced it know that the joy and freedom of being justified in Christ leads a person to hate and shun sin, not embrace it. The wonderful, liberating news of Christ as our substitute *never* implies release from obedience to the law. Forensic righteousness merely frees us from the bondage and futility of trying to be saved by the law.

Atonement is never license to sin, especially on the Day of Atonement, when the people were to "afflict" their souls (see Leviticus 16:31). No matter how adamant they were about justification by faith, the New Testament writers were just as adamant about obedience and a righteous life. "Little children," wrote John, "let no one deceive you. He who practices righteousness is righteous, just as He is righteous" (1 John 3:7). "Those who are Christ's have crucified the flesh with its passions and desires. If we live in the Spirit, let us also walk in the Spirit" (Galatians 5:24, 25).

In the context of the Most Holy Place, where only Christ's righteousness can make atonement, Revelation twice mentions the law (see Revelation 12:17; 14:12). Paul asks, "Do we then make void the law through faith? Certainly not! On the contrary, we establish the law" (Romans 3:31). Those under the delusion that righteousness by faith doesn't require strict obedience to God's commands will one day find themselves crushed by these words as they come from Christ's own mouth: " 'I never knew you; depart from Me, you who practice lawlessness' " (Matthew 7:23).

Neither does the fact that Christ is our substitute negate a judgment based on our works. On the contrary, our works show that we have a saving faith. "Thus also faith by itself, if it does not have works, is dead. But someone will say, 'You have faith, and I have works.' Show me your faith without your works, *and I will show you my faith by my works*" (James 2:17, 18, emphasis supplied).

Non-Adventists see it as well. "Paul's focus on relationship to Christ," writes S. H. Travis in *Dictionary of Paul and His Letters*, "is not in conflict with his affirmation of judgment according to works. For he understands people's deeds as evidence of their character, showing whether their relationship to God is fundamentally one of faith or of unbelief. . . . At the final judgment, the evidence of their deeds will confirm the reality of this relationship."[13] Travis sounds as if he's describing the investigative judgment!

When Revelation 11:19 opens the way into the Most Holy Place of the heavenly sanctuary, it opens the way into the final phase of Christ's work for us. That work is more atonement than judgment, which is why it's called the Day of *Atonement*, not the Day of *Judgment*. Biblical atonement is God's act reconciling us to Himself, and any action devoted exclusively to that reconciliation must be good news. Atonement is always good news; it's the essence of the gospel; and on the Day of Atonement it becomes the best news yet.

---

1. Kenneth Strand, "An Overlooked Old-Testament Background to Revelation 11:1" (*Andrews University Seminary Studies*, 22, no. 3), argues that Revelation 11:1 could itself be linked to the Day of Atonement in Leviticus 16. He sees the "measurement" of the temple, the altar, and the worshipers tied into the *Yom Kippur* ritual. "There is, however, one Old Testament passage that stands in striking parallel with Revelation 11:1—namely, *Leviticus 16*, the description of the ancient Israelite Day of Atonement. With the exception of the omission of the priesthood in Revelation 11:1, the same three elements under review are common to both passages: temple, altar, and worshipers" (324). The problem with this thesis, however, is that Revelation 11:2 seems to have the Holy City being trodden underfoot for "forty and two months" *after* the measuring that takes place in verse 1, which is not the ac-

cepted understanding of Seventh-day Adventists regarding the relationship between the antitypical Day of Atonement and the prophetic time frame depicted by the forty-two months.

2. The transition in Revelation from the Holy Place to the Most Holy Place is paralleled in Daniel 8, which is suffused with sanctuary words and images. A major portion of Daniel 8 deals with the work of the little horn power against the high-priestly ministry of Christ. Daniel makes it clear that the little horn attacks the "*tamid*," the "daily" (verse 11), which is the focus of the heavenly High Priest's first apartment ministry.

"A study of the usages of *tamid* in the book of Leviticus," writes Angel Rodriguez, "discloses that the term was intimately linked with the ministry of the priests in the first apartment of the sanctuary. It is never used in connection with the second-apartment ministry."

Thus, just like the first three heavenly-sanctuary scenes in Revelation, the emphasis in Daniel 8 is on the first apartment only. Yet, as in Revelation, the shift to the next apartment happens in Daniel as well. Daniel 8:14 reads: "For two thousand three hundred days, then the sanctuary shall be cleansed." The link to the Day of Atonement, the second apartment, is obvious because only then—when the High Priest went into the second apartment (which contained the "ark of his testimony")—was the sanctuary cleansed. The chapter moves from the Holy Place to the Most Holy Place. Thus, Daniel 8 does in one chapter what Revelation does in eleven: it covers the transition from the Holy Place to the Most Holy Place.

3. The elements of Daniel 8 itself prove the importance of the pre-advent judgment. The chapter consists of the vision of the ram (verse 3), the male goat (verse 5), the little horn (verse 9), and the sanctuary being cleansed (verse 14). The rest of the chapter explains that vision, or at least most of it.

The ram is identified as Media-Persia (verse 20), one of the most important powers in the ancient world. Its importance can hardly be overemphasized, especially because it was the nation that the Lord used not only to overthrow Babylon but to restore the Jews to their land after the Babylonian captivity. Thus, not only in ancient near-eastern history, but specifically in biblical and even salvation history, Media-Persia was a major player of extreme importance.

The male goat is identified as Greece (verse 21). Again, Daniel is dealing with a player of major significance in history. The Macedonian Greeks, under Alexander, extended their empire across the known ancient world. With Greece, as with Media-Persia, Daniel was dealing with a power and with events of incredible significance.

The little horn is Rome, both pagan and papal. Here, too, the importance of this power cannot be overemphasized, not only for world history but for salvation history as well. We are living not only with the effects of that power, but *we are living with that power today*. According to the Bible (Daniel 2 in particular), these are still the days of the Roman Empire—in its papal phase. It was Rome that crucified Christ; it was Rome that first suppressed and then usurped the gospel; and it's Rome that will have a major role in last-day events. Clearly, that little horn, too, is of great importance.

And finally, the vision of Daniel 8 climaxes with the sanctuary being cleansed in verse 14.

These four elements compose the vision of Daniel 8: Media-Persia, Greece, Rome, and the cleansing of the sanctuary. If the first element, Media-Persia, was so important; and if the second one, Greece, was so important; and if the third, Rome, was and still is so important—what does that prove about the fourth element?

It must be crucial too! If only four elements exist, and the first three are of major importance, the fourth—the cleansing of the sanctuary—must be as well.

Why would the Lord have *climaxed* these three major world powers with an event that itself wasn't also of crucial significance?

However anyone may interpret the cleansing of the sanctuary in Daniel 8:14, it clearly must be a milestone in salvation history, on a par with the major world powers that share the vision with it. And no doubt, the pre-advent judgment, the final judgment before the second coming of Christ, is such an event.

Also, with the application of the day-year principle, which the prophecy itself demands, the 2,300 years of Daniel 8:14 are the longest prophetic time sequence in Scripture. No other prophecy covers as many years. "The fact that God by his prophet appointed the time for the cleansing of the sanctuary more than two thousand years before it was to take place," writes R. F. Cottrell, "clearly indicates that it is an event of no trivial importance. It must be an event of such magnitude as to deeply concern the human race."

The importance of Daniel 8:14 firmly establishes the prophetic calling of Seventh-day Adventism because no one else does anything with it. Most churches ignore the prophecy, and the few that might make any comment about it at all usually link it to an ancient Seleucid king, named Antiochus IV Epiphanes, an absurd interpretation based on false tradition, faulty history, and poor exegesis. The cleansing of the sanctuary is clearly an apocalyptic event of importance unsurpassed by anything except the second coming itself, and Seventh-day Adventists alone know that it's happening, much less preach about it.

It's not a coincidence, either, that at the time of this transition from the Holy Place to the Most Holy Place—1844—the present-truth message linked with it surfaced. The three angels' messages of Revelation 14 began to be preached only after the truth of Christ's second-apartment ministry was understood, because the three angels' messages are tied to that second phase of Christ's work.

4. "None could fail to see that if the earthly sanctuary was a figure or pattern of the heavenly, the law deposited in the ark on earth was an exact transcript of the law in the ark in heaven; and that the acceptance of the truth concerning the heavenly sanctuary involved an acknowledgement of the claims of God's law and the obligation of the Sabbath of the fourth commandment. Here was the secret of the bitter and determined opposition to the harmonious exposition of the Scriptures that revealed the ministration of Christ in the heavenly sanctuary" *(The Great Controversy*, 435).

5. Heppenstall, *Our High Priest*, 219, 220.

6. For the most detailed and comprehensive critique, see Desmond Ford, *Daniel 8:14, The Day of Atonement, and the Investigative Judgment* (Casselberry, Fla.: Euanglion Press, 1980).

7. For a detailed study on Azazel, see Alberto Trieyer, *The Day of Atonement and the Heavenly Judgment*, 231-265.

8. "For it is not possible that the blood of bulls and goats could take away sins" (Hebrews 10:4).

9. See Revelation 3:5; Matthew 10:32; Luke 12:8; Matthew 22:1-13.

10. "When in the typical service the high priest left the holy on the Day of Atonement, he went in before God to present the blood of the sin offering in behalf of all Israel who truly repented of their sins. So Christ had only completed one part of His work as our intercessor, to enter upon another portion of the work, and *He still pleaded His blood before the Father in behalf of sinners*" (*The Great Controversy,* 429, emphasis supplied).

11. Norman Gulley, "Daniel's Pre-Advent Judgment in Its Biblical Context," *Journal of the Adventist Theological Society* (Autumn 1991, 59).

12. *Strong's Exhaustive Concordance* has a version of *kpr* used for every translation of the word "atonement" in the Old Testament.

13. S. H. Travis, "Judgment," in *Dictionary of Paul and His Letters*, Gerald Hawthorne and Ralph Martin, eds. (Downers Grove, Ill.: InterVarsity Press, 1993), 517.

Chapter
Nine

ONE LIKE THE SON OF MAN

How unfortunate that for more than a century Christ's work in the second apartment of the sanctuary in heaven has been twisted, so that instead of seeing the pre-advent judgment as the climactic application of Calvary in our behalf, many Adventists have put the judgment in tension with, even in opposition to, the cross. Salvation should have been rooted in what Christ has done for us, yet we have taught the investigative judgment in such a way that we have focused attention upon ourselves and how well we have performed—a hopeless prospect for even the holiest and most sanctified Seventh-day Adventist Christian.

No wonder so many Adventists don't have assurance of salvation. How could anyone have hope who is looking to herself and her deeds to make her acceptable to God—especially if she has also glimpsed the holiness and righteousness of the Deity? Far from negating the gospel, however, Christ's ministry in the Most Holy Place of the heavenly sanctuary, *when taught in relationship to what He accomplished at the cross*, affirms that our salvation comes only from faith in what He has done for us and nothing else.

"There are no exceptions to the gospel," writes Helmut Ott. "He who has the Son has eternal life; he who does not have the Son does not have eternal life. We are saved by grace through faith in the Saviour's merits, or we are not saved at all."[1]

Also, some Adventists downplay the concept of two apartments in the heavenly sanctuary—no doubt in response to the poor way in general that we have taught the idea of the judgment. Though these faithful Adventists believe in the existence of the sanctuary, the truth of the investigative judgment, and the validity of 1844, they nevertheless reject the idea of Christ moving His ministry from the Holy Place to the Most Holy Place of the heavenly sanctuary. Instead, they focus on the *phases* of Christ's heavenly ministry rather than on a celestial movement.[2]

Of course, the phases of Christ's ministry matter infinitely more than the motion. What's crucial is what Christ does in heaven, not how. Nevertheless, this new emphasis, although perhaps a well-meaning attempt to make the doctrine more palatable to non-Adventists, not only departs from what the pioneers taught,[3] but is really an unnecessary concession.

Does Christ actually move from one apartment to another in the heavenly sanctuary?

A good place to start is Daniel, chapter 7. This chapter begins on earth, with four great beasts, representative of four world kingdoms arising out of "the Great Sea" (verse 2). The lion, bear, leopard, and fourth beast have been interpreted for centuries by both Jewish and Christian biblical scholars as the successive kingdoms of Babylon, Media-Persia, Greece, and pagan Rome.[4]

Next, out of the pagan Roman beast sprouted a ferocious little-horn power that would, among other things, make "war against the saints" (verse 21), "speak pompous words against the Most High" (verse 25), and "intend to change times and law" (verse 25). This little horn was further delineated by a prophetic time prophecy that placed an aspect of its work into the eighteenth or nineteenth century.[5]

Many modern scholars identify this little-horn power as the Seleucid king Antiochus Epiphanes (second century B.C.).[6] Futurists identify it as an unknown power yet to arise. Yet the characteristics of this little horn, as given in Scripture, prove that it can be only papal Rome, as numerous Jewish and Christian scholars have recognized for centuries.[7]

After describing the little-horn power, the emphasis of the chapter shifts upward to the judgment scene in heaven. Three times in Daniel, chapter 7 this judgment appears.

"I beheld till the thrones were *cast down*, and the Ancient of days did sit" (verse 9, KJV). The verse then describes the Ancient of days—"whose garment was white as snow, and the hair of his head like the pure wool"—as well as His throne: "His throne was like the fiery flame, and his wheels as burning fire." The next verse depicts a vast heavenly throng who "stood before him," and finally, "the judgment was set, and the books were opened" (verse 10, KJV).

Verse 9 says that the thrones "were cast down." The root of this Aramaic verb, *rma*, means literally "to throw" or "to cast." The same root appears in Daniel 3:24, when Nebuchadnezzar asked his soldiers, "Did we not *cast* three men bound into the midst of the fire?" (KJV) and in Daniel 6:16, when "they brought Daniel, and *cast* him into the den of lions" (KJV). Why this particular verb was employed in Daniel 7:9 is another story,[8] but the important point is that these thrones, being "cast down," are in motion.

Daniel's description of God's throne in connection with the judgment reflects Ezekiel's imagery when he describes his vision of the Lord also on a throne (see Ezekiel 1:26), surrounded with flames (verse 4), and with wheels (verse 16). Though the context of Ezekiel differs from Daniel, in both cases, the throne, or thrones, move.[9]

This judgment scene continues in Daniel 7:13. "I saw in the night visions, and, behold, one like the Son of man *came* with the clouds of heaven, and *came* to the Ancient of days, and they *brought* him near before him" (KJV).

This "Son of Man"[10] is, of course, Jesus, who in each of the four Gospels calls Himself the "Son of Man."[11] The "clouds of heaven" may be understood as angels, which en masse appear as clouds.[12] And, despite far-fetched higher critical attempts to link the "Ancient of days" to the Canaanite god El,[13] this phrase clearly refers to the Father, Yahweh Himself, the "eternal God."[14]

In verse 13, the three verbs that refer to the "Son of man" in Daniel's vision each denote movement.

The verse says the Son of man *"came* with the clouds of heaven" (emphasis supplied). The Aramaic root of the verb *ath* means literally "come." It is used, for example, in Ezra 5:3, "At the same time *came* to them Tatnai, governor on this side the river," and in Ezra 4:12, "Be it known unto the king, that the Jews which *came* up from thee to us are come unto Jerusalem" (KJV, emphasis supplied).

Daniel 7:13 further says that the Son of man "*came* to the Ancient days" (emphasis supplied). This verb is from the root *mth*, which means "to reach." It is used in Daniel 6:24, referring to Daniel's accusers who were thrust into the lions' den and devoured as soon as they "*came* at [from *mth*, meaning "reached"] the bottom of the den" (KJV, emphasis supplied).

The last phrase in Daniel 7:13 says of the Son of man that "they *brought* him near before him [the Ancient of days]" (emphasis supplied). The verb *brought* comes from *qrb*, which means "to approach." It is used in Daniel 6:12, "Then they *came near* [from *qrb*, meaning "approached"] and spake before the king" (KJV, emphasis supplied). In Daniel 7:13, *qrb* appears in a special form that means "to cause to come near," or in clearer English, "to bring near." Thus, "they [the clouds of heaven, or angels] brought him [the Son of man] near before him [the Ancient of days]" (verse 13, KJV).

Clearly, these three action verbs in verse 13 describe the motion of the Son of man.

And finally, Daniel 7:22 reads: "Until the Ancient of days *came*, and judgment was given to the saints of the most High; and the time came that the saints possessed the kingdom" (KJV). Here, too, the verb used in connection with the Ancient of days is from the Aramaic root *ath*, meaning "to come." *Obviously, the Ancient of days Himself was in motion.*

These verses depict different aspects of the pre-advent judgment. Although not given in chronological order, the events could be constructed like this: "The Ancient of days came" (verse 22), and then "thrones were cast down [placed], and the Ancient of days did sit" (verse 9, KJV). Next, one "like the Son of man came with the clouds of heaven, and came to the Ancient of days" (verse 13, KJV). The "judgment was set, and the books were opened" (verse 10, KJV). And, finally, "the time came that the saints possessed the kingdom" (verse 22, KJV).

Whatever the order, *motion*—whether it be the thrones, the

99

angels, Jesus, or the Father—is indisputable.

Thus, with motion so clearly depicted in Daniel's description of the pre-advent judgment, why should we have a problem with Jesus moving from the Holy Place to the Most Holy Place of the heavenly sanctuary? The judgment scene itself, as given in Daniel, chapter 7, says nothing about the sanctuary. But the description of the judgment in Daniel, chapter 7 is parallel to Daniel 8:14, which is about nothing but the sanctuary. The judgment in Daniel 7 and the cleansing of the sanctuary in Daniel 8 are the same event—just shown from different perspectives. And Daniel's perspective in chapter 7 clearly shows the movement involved.

Exodus shows that the earthly type had two apartments; Leviticus shows that the High Priest went into the Most Holy Place when it was cleansed; Hebrews shows that Christ is now our High Priest in the heavenly sanctuary; Daniel 8 shows that the heavenly sanctuary is cleansed; Revelation shows the way into the Most Holy Place of the heavenly sanctuary; and Daniel shows clearly the motion involved in the judgment. So it seems clear that "the Son of man" went into the Most Holy Place of the heavenly sanctuary on the antitypical Day of Atonement.

Ellen White adds some interesting insights into the motion involved in the pre-advent judgment. She wrote in *Early Writings*:

I saw a throne and on it sat the Father and the Son. I saw the Father rise from the throne, and in a flaming chariot go into the holy of holies within the veil and sit down. Then Jesus rose up from the throne, and most of those who were bowed down arose with Him. I did not see one ray of light pass from Jesus to the careless multitude after He arose, and they were left in darkness. Those who arose when Jesus did, kept their eyes fixed on Him as He left the throne and led them out a little way. Then He raised His right arm, and we heard His lovely voice saying, "Wait here; I am going to my Father to receive the kingdom; keep your garments spotless, and in a little while I will return from the wedding and receive you to Myself." Then a cloudy chariot, with wheels like flaming fire, surrounded by angels, came to where Jesus was. He stepped into the chariot and was borne to the holiest, where the Father sat.[15]

Ellen White describes here, from another angle, the same event Daniel describes in chapter 7. In Daniel 7, the "Ancient of days" moves and does "sit" (verse 9). In Ellen White's vision, she saw the Father move into the Holy of Holies and then "sit down."

Next, in Daniel 7, "one like the Son of man came with the clouds of heaven, and came to the Ancient of days" (verse 13, KJV). In Ellen White's vision, she describes a "cloudy chariot" that took Jesus "to the holiest, where the Father sat."

Also, in Daniel 7, it was the clouds of heaven that brought Jesus to the Father (see verse 13); in Ellen White's vision, she sees a "cloudy chariot" bring Jesus to the Father.

In Daniel 7, after both Jesus and the Father have moved, the "saints possessed the kingdom" (verse 22, KJV). In Ellen White's vision, Jesus said that He was going to His Father "to receive the kingdom."

Clearly, Daniel and Ellen White are describing the same event; it's the same vision. Ellen White sees Jesus first with the Father. Where had Jesus been before the 2300 days were completed? Hebrews depicts Jesus as being in the sanctuary in heaven, the "true tabernacle" (8:2), two thousand years ago. In *Early Writings*, Ellen White pictures Jesus in the sanctuary, too, next to the Father. If both the Father and the Son are together, and if both don't go into the Most Holy Place until the end of the 2300 days, then where is the only place They both were before the 2300 days ended? It must be the Holy Place. Ellen White wrote, "I saw the Father rise from the *throne*." Was the throne, then, in the Holy Place? Obviously.

Scholars generally want to place God's throne in the Most Holy Place only—the idea being that where God is, that's where His throne must be, a fair-enough position.[16] Yet the supposition that God's presence must always be in the Most Holy Place is just that, a supposition. Though He is often depicted in the Most Holy Place, nothing in Scripture demands that His pres-

101

ence be manifested only there.

"The assumption," writes Mervyn Maxwell, "that God's celestial throne is located only in the heavenly Most Holy Place overlooks the fact that in Old Testament times God's presence was not always confined to the Most Holy Place but was sometimes represented in the Holy Place."[17]

Exodus 33:9 states that "the pillar of cloud descended and stood at the door of the tabernacle, and the Lord talked with Moses." Deuteronomy 31:15 places God in the same location—at the door of the tabernacle. Ezekiel 9:3 describes "the glory of the God of Israel" at "the threshold of the temple." Exodus 40:34 depicts the "glory of the Lord" filling the entire tabernacle. Although God's usual location in connection with the sanctuary service was the Most Holy Place, the Bible doesn't limit Him only to that spot. Thus, again, the idea that God the Father and Jesus Christ move from the Holy Place to the Most Holy Place of the heavenly sanctuary doesn't contradict Scripture.[18]

Some argue that Daniel's vision of heavenly judgment is only symbolic. Yet is the Ancient of Days symbolic? Is the Son of man symbolic? Or the numerous beings watching the judgment? Certainly the Father and Son are real, so why shouldn't the motion surrounding them be as well?

Others have a problem with the idea of placing God in a "box" in heaven. But why? After all, He managed to manifest Himself between the cherubim in the Most Holy Place of the earthly tabernacle—a specific location. Why should we have a problem picturing Him residing in the "greater and more perfect" tabernacle (Hebrews 9:11)? Certainly it should be harder to conceive of God placing Himself between two gold angels in an earthly structure than among thousands and thousands of real angels in a heavenly edifice.

Also, what can be harder to imagine than the Creator's stepping out of infinity and eternity and tabernacling in human flesh? If Jesus—the One who "is before all things, and in Him all things consist" (Colossians 1:17)—could manifest Himself in the world as a helpless infant, why should there be any problem with God's manifesting Himself in the heavenly sanctuary? The problem is not with the doctrine of the Father and Christ ministering in a two-apartment sanctuary in heaven but with those whose imagination limits God.

Adventists have long claimed that the judgment is for the benefit of the onlooking universe, which, though intensely interested in the issues of sin and salvation, lacks the foreknowledge or omnipotence of the Father. "The investigation is not conducted for the information of God or of Christ," says the *SDA Bible Commentary*, "but for the information of the universe at large—that God may be vindicated in accepting some and rejecting others."[19] Thus, the sanctuary, the books, the thrones, even the judgment itself are all on display for these "heavenly intelligences,"[20] which at least suggests that these are literal elements.

Most importantly, the motion in the courts above shows that God is not static, that He is not involved in human history only at a certain point and then leaves humans to their own fate. On the contrary, God is a living, dynamic power constantly in touch, and interacting, with His creation, particularly His redeemed, even today.

Daniel, Hebrews, and Revelation teach that salvation is God's ongoing activity. The Lord remains directly involved in our redemption now. His ministry as High Priest in the sanctuary above is the constant application for us now of what He has done as Lamb here below. Heaven is, indeed, astir with the redemptive, saving activity of God on our behalf. No wonder Jesus said, "Look up and lift up your heads, because your redemption draws near" (Luke 21:28). We should be looking upward by faith to Christ our High Priest ministering in the heavenly sanctuary.

"Therefore He is also able to save to the uttermost those who come to God through Him, since He ever lives to make intercession for them" (Hebrews 7:25).

---

1. Helmut Ott, "Another Look at Valuegenesis," *Ministry* (February 1994, 20).

2. For the most recent example of this type of thinking, see Roy Adams, *The Sanctuary* (Review and Herald, 1993). Even the language of the Twenty-seven Fundamental Beliefs gives this emphasis. "There

is a sanctuary in heaven, the true tabernacle which the Lord set up and not man. In it Christ ministers in our behalf, making available to believers the benefits of His atoning sacrifice offered once and for all on the cross. He was inaugurated as our great High Priest and began His intercessory ministry at the time of His ascension. In 1844, at the end of the prophetic period or 2300 days, He entered the second and last *phase* of His work" (emphasis supplied).

3. For example, Uriah Smith wrote (*Review and Herald*, 18 February 1858) that "here, then, Paul calls the tabernacle erected by Moses a *shadow* of heavenly things. One distinguishing feature of this tabernacle was that it had two apartments, a holy and a most holy place. The heavenly sanctuary has the same; for a sanctuary in heaven with only one apartment would not cast a shadow upon earth with two."

J. N. Andrews wrote (*Review and Herald*, 3 February 1853) that "the temple was built on a larger and grander scale than the tabernacle; but its distinguishing feature, like the tabernacle, consisted in the fact that it was composed of two holy places. This is clear proof that the heavenly tabernacle contains the same."

James White wrote (*Review and Herald*, 8 September 1863) that "an examination of this subject would have shown us that the cleansing of the sanctuary which was then to take place, signified merely that our great High Priest would change his ministration from the holy to the most holy of the heavenly temple, there to finish up his work of mediation for the world."

"Therefore the announcement that the temple of God was opened in heaven and the ark of His testament was seen points to the opening of the most holy place of the heavenly sanctuary in 1844 as Christ entered there to perform the closing work of atonement. Those who by faith followed their great High Priest as He entered upon His ministry in the most holy place, beheld the ark of His testament" (*The Great Controversy*, 433).

For a comprehensive compilation of what the pioneers wrote about the sanctuary, see *Pioneer Articles on the Sanctuary, Daniel 8:14, the Judgment, the 2300 Days, Year-Day Principle, Atonement, 1846-1905*, compiled by Paul Gordon, 1983.

4. See L. E. Froom, *Prophetic Faith of Our Fathers* (Washington, D. C.: Review and Herald, 1953).

5. For more details on this aspect of the time prophecy, see William Shea, *Selected Studies on Prophetic Interpretation* (Washington, D.C.: Review and Herald, 1982), 56-88.

6. Louis Hartman and Alexander Di Lella, *The Book of Daniel* (Garden City, N.Y.: Doubleday and Company, Inc., 1977).

7. Hartman and Di Lella, *Book of Daniel,* 3.

8. William Shea, "Unity of Daniel," in *Symposium on Daniel* (Silver Spring, Md.: Biblical Research Institute, 1986), 210-216.

9. See Shea, *Selected Studies on Prophetic Interpretation*, 13-20.

10. Arthur Ferch, *The Son of Man in Daniel 7* (Berrien Springs, Mich.: Andrews University Press, 1979).

11. See Matthew 25:31; 26:2; Mark 2:8; 9:9; Luke 9:22; John 3:13, 14.

12. See also Acts 1:9; Revelation 1:7; Matthew 24:30.

13. Frank Cross, *Canaanite Myth and Hebrew Epic* (Cambridge, Mass.: Harvard University Press, 1973), 17.

14. Judah Slotki, *Daniel, Ezra, Nehemiah* (London: Soncino Press, 1978), 58.

15. *Early Writings*, 54.

16. See, for example, Mario Veloso, "The Doctrine of the Sanctuary and the Atonement in the Book of Revelation," in *The Sanctuary and the Atonement: Biblical, Historical, and Theological Studies*, A. V. Wallenkampf and W. R. Lesher, eds. (Washington, D.C.: Biblical Research Institute, 1981), 394-419.

17. C. Mervyn Maxwell, *God Cares*, vol. 2 (Boise, Idaho: Pacific Press, 1985), 172.

18. In chapter 4, I discussed the Daniel and Revelation Committee's conclusion that the heavenly introductory scene of Revelation, chapters 4 and 5 is the inauguration of the heavenly sanctuary. While I agree, this view was argued for partially on the basis that the scene contained imagery from "nearly every aspect of the Hebrew cultus," including the Most Holy Place, brought specifically to view by John's vision of the "throne." Yet the throne itself doesn't have to be in the Most Holy Place. In fact, if the throne is in the Most Holy Place, this destroys the concept that the first half of Revelation, at least to chapter 11, deals with the first-apartment ministry, because the throne is seen in numerous other verses before Revelation 11. (See Revelation 6:13; 7:11, 15, 17; 8:3.) How, then, could this part of the Apocalypse deal only with the first apartment? On the other hand, if the Father moves (as He does in Daniel 7), and His throne follows, the problem is solved. The throne scenes prior to Revelation, chapter 11 are in the Holy Place. Meanwhile, Revelation, chapters 4 and 5 can still be an

inauguration scene, even if the focus is on the Holy Place only.
    19. *SDA Bible Commentary*, 4:828.
    20. See *Testimonies for the Church*, 6:316.

Chapter
Ten

THE TABERNACLE OF THE TESTIMONY

The previous heavenly-sanctuary scene dealt with a judgment in heaven. The next sanctuary scene—Revelation 15:5–16:1—deals with a judgment on earth, the judgment of the seven last plagues:

> After these things I looked, and behold, *the temple of the tabernacle of the testimony in heaven* was opened. And out of *the temple* came the seven angels having the seven plagues, clothed in pure bright linen, and having their chests girded with golden bands. Then one of the four living creatures gave to the seven angels seven golden bowls full of the wrath of God who lives forever and ever. *The temple* was filled with smoke from the glory of God and from His power, and no one was able to enter *the temple* till the seven plagues of the seven angels were completed (Revelation 15:5-8, emphasis supplied).

Immediately after this heavenly scene, Revelation describes the devastation of the plagues on earth: sores, scorchings, darkness, etc. These verses emphasize what all of Revelation makes obvious: that events in heaven cause events on earth. "Then I heard a loud voice *from the temple* saying to the seven angels, 'Go and pour out the bowls of the wrath of God *on the earth*' " (Revelation 16:1, emphasis supplied).

What has happened in heaven that would cause such dire consequences on earth?

In Revelation 15:5–16:1, the temple is mentioned five times. John sees the temple in heaven opened. The angels carrying the plagues leave the temple. Smoke fills the temple, and no one can enter the temple until the plagues are completed. Finally, a voice from the temple orders the angels to pour out the plagues.

The most instructive delineation of the temple in these verses is the first. John says, "After these things I looked, and behold, the temple of *the tabernacle of the testimony* in heaven was opened" (Revelation 15:5, emphasis supplied). The "tabernacle of the testimony" is not a common expression. It appears only five times in Scripture, and other than here in Revelation 15, the phrase occurs only in Exodus and Numbers. "You shall appoint the Levites over the tabernacle of the Testimony, over all its furnishings, and over all things that belong to it" (Numbers 1:50).[1]

The "testimony," of course, repeatedly refers to the law of God,[2] the Ten Commandments, which in the context of the sanctuary appear only in the Most Holy Place. Although it is tempting to assert that this sanctuary scene refers to the Most Holy Place alone (especially since the rest of the vision refers to the "temple" as a whole, rather than to any specific part), the expression "tabernacle of the Testimony" lends itself to the entire sanctuary.

Nevertheless, the phrase does emphasize the law. In contrast to the previous sanctuary vision (Revelation 11:19), which literally reads "the ark of His covenant," Revelation 15:5 reads "the tabernacle of the testimony." The emphasis in the latter phrase is on the testimony, the law. The phrase "the ark of His covenant"—though definitely related to the Most Holy Place (which implies the law)—doesn't place as much focus on the law as does the phrase "the tabernacle of the testimony." The ark of the covenant is the box that contained the testimony; it is *not* the testimony itself.

The difference could be significant. As we saw in the previous chapter, Revelation 11:19 is a view of the investigative judgment, the heavenly Day of Atonement, and the central aspect of atonement is God's work for us. If so, then the emphasis must be on something other than the law, for the law does not, and cannot, atone. The law, specifically our transgressions of it, is what makes atonement necessary. Blood—the symbol of Christ's perfect life—is sprinkled upon the *kapporet*, the "mercy seat," which comes from a word meaning "atonement." Perhaps for this reason John writes in Revelation 11:19 about seeing the "ark of His covenant," with the *kapporet* on the top. This pre-advent judgment scene focuses on the ark, symbol of atonement, rather than "the tabernacle of the *testimony*," symbol of the law.

In Revelation 15:5, however, the emphasis is on the law, not mercy and atonement. Unredeemed humankind must face the consequences of its transgression of that law.

"Once before," writes G. B. Caird, "in the vision of the last trumpet (xi.19), he [John] has seen the same heavenly shrine open and the ark appear. This time it is not the ark but the Testimony it contains which occupies his attention. The time for mercy is over, and God's law must now take its course."[3]

In this fifth sanctuary scene, the "wrath of God" is mentioned three times. As a result of this heavenly activity, the plagues are poured out. The sanctuary is filled with smoke, and no one ("no man" in the King James Version, which often uses this wording to mean an angel)[4] can enter until the plagues are fulfilled. Why the angels specifically can't go into the temple during this time is not clear, but it could imply that the judgment brought to view in Revelation 11:19 has ended. Daniel (with help from Exodus, Leviticus, and Hebrews) shows that during the pre-advent judgment, numerous angelic beings witnessed the judgment in the sanctuary. Daniel 7:10 describes "ten thousand times ten thousand" beings standing before the Lord as "the court was seated, and the books were opened." The books must be for the benefit of these onlooking beings, not for the Lord Himself, who knows all things.

In the last section of Revelation 14 (which immediately precedes John's view of the heavenly sanctuary in chapter 15), the time has come for the wicked to be cast "into the great winepress of the wrath of God" (Revelation 14:19) and for the saved to be "reaped" from the earth (verse 16). The judgment must be over, because the Lord would not be rewarding the righteous and punishing the wicked until He had judged them. And now, until God's wrath is poured out upon the impenitent, none can enter the sanctuary, where myriads of angels had before been witnessing the judgment. The heavenly-sanctuary scene of Revelation 15:5–16:1 shows, then, the end of the pre-advent judgment and the cessation of Christ's mediatorial role as our High Priest.

"The fifth sanctuary scene," writes Davidson, "marks the closing up or 'de-inauguration' of the sanctuary. It is filled with smoke from the glory of God, and no one can enter: probation is closed. The seven last plagues follow, God's wrath unmingled with mercy (16:1-21)."[5]

In Revelation 15:1, John sees the seven angels who have the seven last plagues. Then, as a parenthetical scene, he is shown the redeemed in heaven, "those who have the victory over the beast, over his image and over his mark and over the number of his name" (Revelation 15:2). The vision then proceeds to the sanctuary itself, from which the angels leave and pour out the plagues upon the earth. Every person's case must have been decided, and now God's wrath is poured out upon those who don't have "the seal of God" but rather the "mark of the beast."

Those who have gained the victory over the beast and his image and who sing the song of Moses on the sea of glass are contrasted to those upon whom the plagues fall. The plagues fall on those who "have shed the blood of saints and prophets" (Revelation 16:6), have "blasphemed the name of God" (verse 9), and "did not repent of their deeds" (verse 11). Probation has closed, and they face the wrath of God.[6]

The close of probation and the cessation of Christ's high-priestly ministry depicted here raise numerous controversial questions that no doubt will continue to be debated until the actual close of probation itself: What will God's people be like after probation closes? Will they be sinning? Will they be perfect? What does it mean to live without a mediator? Are these people saved differently from others who have lived in earlier ages?

Much extremism, reactionism, and legalism have resulted from this topic. The problem has often come from the selective use of quotations from the Spirit of Prophecy, each side piling up the statements it believes support its position. Any position, however, particularly on such important topics, should be based on the Bible, not on Ellen White.

Probably the greatest misconception dealing with the close of probation has to do with the salvation of this final group, often called the 144,000. Many Adventist Christians have lost hope, even faith, because of misconceptions regarding this final generation. Hammered with *selected* statements from the Spirit of Prophecy, many have either thrown out the message entirely or have drifted into an "evangelical Adventism" that often leads to an imbalanced gospel.

Such problems wouldn't arise if one point were emphasized in every discussion regarding those who live without a mediator: whoever these people are, whatever their characters, obedience, or holiness—they have no hope of salvation apart from what Christ did for them on the cross two thousand years ago! Like every sinner who has ever lived, they can find salvation only in Christ and His righteousness.

This point can't be stressed enough. Salvation comes only in God's appointed way, and that is through faith in Jesus Christ alone. "Nor is there salvation in any other, for there is no other name under heaven given among men by which we must be saved" (Acts 4:12). "Therefore having been justified by faith, we have peace with God through our Lord Jesus Christ" (Romans 5:1). "Knowing that a man is not justified by the works of the law but by faith in Jesus Christ, even we have believed in Christ Jesus, that we might be justified by faith in Christ and not by the works of the law" (Galatians 2:16). "He who believes in Him is not condemned; but he who does not believe is condemned already, because he has not believed in the name of the only begotten Son of God" (John 3:18).

These truths don't apply only to former generations or only to those who die before the Lord appears and are resurrected. They apply to everyone in every age, even the translated saints at the end of time who live after the judgment is finished and Christ has ceased His intercession in the sanctuary above. The only thing that enables these people to pass through the judgment is the imputed righteousness of Christ. Christ stands in their stead, pleading the merits of His perfection on their behalf one last time.

Indeed, what Christ does *for* us and what He does *in* us, no matter how inseparable in practice, must be kept distinct in our theology. The more one preaches victory, the more one needs to preach justification. The higher one's standards of holiness, the higher he must lift the cross and what it has accomplished. The more one seeks perfection, the more one needs to experience grace. And the more one talks about the final generation that lives without a mediator, the more one must talk about the perfect life of Christ imputed to that final generation.

The issue of those who live through the judgment at the end of time is not—or at least should not be—about how those in that group are saved, though it has often been framed in that context. Everyone is saved in the same way: by the blood of Christ. The issue of perfection is not: How perfect must this final generation be in order to be saved and sealed? Rather, it should be: Now that these people have been saved and sealed by Christ's righteousness, how do they live in response? And that is the very same issue that every redeemed individual has faced throughout the history of sin and salvation.

This concept of *perfection* is often talked about only in the context of the final generation. It is usually debated, not from the Bible, but from Ellen White; whoever has the most quotes wins. However, *perfection* is a biblical term, a biblical concept, even a biblical promise. Biblical perfection isn't limited to those who live without a mediator and who will be translated. It's a biblical promise that has existed in every age; if we understand that, it will help us to understand what perfection means for the final generation.

Almost four thousand years ago, the Lord said to Abraham, "I am the Almighty God; walk before me, and be thou perfect" (Genesis 17:1, KJV).

He told the generation of Hebrews about to enter the Promised Land: "Thou shalt be perfect with the Lord thy God" (Deuteronomy 18:13, KJV).

At the dedication of the temple, King Solomon stood before

his people and said, "Let your heart therefore be perfect with the Lord your God" (1 Kings 8:61, KJV).

Almost 2,900 years ago, the prophet Hanani said to King Asa, "The eyes of the Lord run to and fro throughout the whole earth, to shew himself strong in behalf of them whose heart is perfect toward him" (2 Chronicles 16:9, KJV).

Said the psalmist: "I will behave myself wisely in a perfect way. O when wilt thou come unto me? I will walk within my house with a perfect heart" (Psalm 101:2, KJV).

Jesus believed in perfection: "Be ye therefore perfect, even as your Father which is in heaven is perfect" (Matthew 5:48, KJV).

Paul wrote: "Having therefore these promises, dearly beloved, let us cleanse ourselves from all filthiness of the flesh and spirit, perfecting holiness in the fear of God" (2 Corinthians 7:1, KJV).

Not as though I had already attained, either were already perfect: but I follow after, if that I may apprehend [attain] that for which also I am apprehended of Christ Jesus. Brethren, I count not myself to have apprehended: but this one thing I do, forgetting those things which are behind, and reaching forth unto those things which are before, I press toward the mark for the prize of the high calling of God in Christ Jesus. Let us therefore, as many as be perfect, be thus minded: and if in any thing ye be otherwise minded, God shall reveal even this unto you (Philippians 3:12-15, KJV).

"Whom we preach, warning every man, and teaching every man in all wisdom; that we may present every man perfect in Christ Jesus" (Colossians 1:28, KJV).

"Epaphras, who is one of you, a servant of Christ, saluteth you, always laboring fervently for you in prayers, that ye may stand perfect and complete in all the will of God" (Colossians 4:12, KJV).

"Therefore leaving the principles of the doctrine of Christ, let us go on unto perfection" (Hebrews 6:1, KJV).

"Let patience have her perfect work, that ye may be perfect and entire—wanting nothing" (James 1:4, KJV).

"I have not found thy works perfect before God" (Revelation 3:2, KJV).

Obviously, biblical perfection is not an Adventist doctrine derived only from the writings of Ellen White and applicable only to the final generation. God has been calling people to perfection for thousands of years!

Among these was Noah. "Noah was a just man and *perfect* in his generations, and Noah walked with God" (Genesis 6:9, KJV, emphasis supplied). Of course, Noah didn't do such a great job with his children, and this "perfect" man did once get drunk and make an idiot of himself.

"It came to pass, when Solomon was old, that his wives turned away his heart after other gods: and his heart was not *perfect* with the Lord his God, as was the heart of David his father" (1 Kings 11:4, KJV, emphasis supplied). Despite adultery, murder, lying, indulging his children, and polygamy—David was perfect?

The Bible says that "the heart of [King] Asa was perfect all his days" (2 Chronicles 15:17, KJV); it then tells about his illicit league with Syrian king Benhadad, the rebuke that it brought him from Hanani the prophet, and the king's response: "Then Asa was wroth with the seer, and put him in a prison house; for he was in a rage with him because of this thing. And Asa oppressed some of the people the same time" (2 Chronicles 16:10, KJV).

Obviously, biblical perfection doesn't mean sinlessness, never making a mistake, or never falling short of God's ideal.[7] That's why all these "perfect" men needed the righteousness of Christ imputed to them in order to be saved—just as has everyone else who has ever lived.

Biblical perfection must mean attitude, not actions, because the actions of these men were hardly perfect, nor were their works flawless.

"Let your heart therefore be perfect with the Lord our God" (1 Kings 8:61, KJV). "His [Solomon's] heart was not perfect with the Lord his God, as was the heart of David his father" (1 Kings 11:4, KJV). "The eyes of the Lord run to and fro throughout the whole earth, to shew himself strong in behalf of them whose

114

heart is perfect toward him" (2 Chronicles 16:9, KJV).

It's the heart that God sees. "For the Lord seeth not as man seeth; for man looketh on the outward appearance, but the LORD looketh on the heart" (1 Samuel 16:7, KJV). We can't be saved by what we do, because works of the law can never be good enough to merit salvation. In contrast, faith is a work of the heart—and that is what determines our standing with God: "Therefore we conclude that a man is justified by faith apart from the deeds of the law" (Romans 3:28).

When Jesus said to the rich young ruler, " 'If you want to be *perfect*, go, sell what you have and give to the poor' " (Matthew 19:21), did He mean that if this man merely sold his goods and gave his wealth to the poor, he would then be ethically flawless, sinless, and would never make a mistake, never need to repent again, never do anything else wrong, but constantly show perfect love, compassion, and mercy? Of course not. The problem with the rich young ruler was his heart. He needed an attitude adjustment. He had one thing—one idol—that he was clinging to, and once he got rid of it, he would be totally committed, and thus "perfect" in God's sight.

The Lord wants our hearts, because then our deeds and actions will follow. Though Noah, David, and Asa did make mistakes, their "perfect" heart toward God was manifested in holy actions. Despite the notable exceptions in their lives that Scripture delineates (and how many more not recorded?), these men were faithful, obedient believers in Christ, and it showed in repentance, holiness, and obedience. Even David, with the most egregious sins, displayed instant repentance when confronted by Nathan. His heart was right with God, even if his actions sometimes weren't.

"I will behave myself wisely in a perfect way. Oh when will you come to me? I will walk within my house with a perfect heart" (Psalm 101:2). What sinner ever walked "in a perfect way," in the sense of never making a mistake, never having a wrong thought, always showing perfect love and compassion, always praying the perfect amount of time, always doing everything perfectly? Walking in "a perfect way" means walking with a perfect heart, a heart that is totally committed to God, because if our heart is right with God, our actions—at whatever stage we may be in our spiritual growth—will be right too.

Perfection is a relative term. A person whose heart has been perfect with God for only three years should not be expected to act the same as one whose heart has been perfect for thirty years. In Hebrews 9:11, for example, the Bible talks about "a greater and more perfect tabernacle." How can something be "more perfect" unless perfection (the Greek word means "mature") is relative?[8] A newborn baby might be all that a baby is expected to be, but at two weeks old it's nowhere near the flutist or the engineer that it may someday be. Thus, in the sight of God, we can be perfect while we are still pressing toward perfection.

However, this understanding of biblical perfection still doesn't answer the question of what happens in Revelation 15, when probation closes and the wrath of God is poured out without mercy upon the wicked. What happens in that fearful time when the righteous must live in the sight of a holy God without a mediator?[9] After all, no matter how perfect your heart might be toward God, if you did what David did, you'd need a mediator! "My little children, these things I write to you, that you may not sin. And if anyone sins, we have an Advocate with the Father, Jesus Christ the righteous" (1 John 2:1).

What happens when we no longer have an Advocate with the Father? "He saw that there was no man, and wondered that there was no intercessor" (Isaiah 59:16). If Revelation 15 depicts the close of probation and the end of Christ's high-priestly ministry, what are His faithful followers like who live at that time?

Again, the issue here is *not* salvation. These people have already been sealed in Christ, vindicated in the judgment by His righteousness pleaded on their behalf. No matter how holy and righteous they are or how fully they reflect the image of Jesus, their only hope is in what Christ did for them on the cross.

"God has only one criterion for salvation:" writes Beatrice S. Neall, "faith in the merits of a crucified Saviour. Justification alone is our title to heaven. For God to change the requirements on the last generation would be unjust."[10]

Nevertheless, Scripture teaches about a purified final generation. We don't need Ellen White to prove that God will have a holy and righteous people in the last days.

" 'He who is unjust, let him be unjust still; he who is filthy, let him be filthy still; he who is righteous, let him be righteous still; he who is holy, let him be holy still' " (Revelation 22:11).

This text must deal with the close of probation, because only then would God leave the unjust and filthy to their ways without offering them the hope of repentance and salvation.

But just as the unjust and filthy are at this time, indeed, unjust and filthy, so those who are holy and righteous are, indeed, holy and righteous. This isn't just a legal declaration; it is an existential fact.

"Little children, let no one deceive you. He who practices righteousness is righteous, just as He is righteous" (1 John 3:7). "Having these promises, beloved, let us cleanse ourselves from all filthiness of the flesh and spirit, perfecting holiness in the fear of God" (2 Corinthians 7:1). "Pursue peace with all men, and holiness, without which no one will see the Lord" (Hebrews 12:14).

Holiness and righteousness aren't just objective declarations in heaven; they are subjective experiences in the lives of all Christ's true followers, even though not everyone will reach the same level. If sanctification is the work of a lifetime, then clearly Christ can do more in some lives than in others. And, no doubt, Jesus has the opportunity to develop His righteousness to a greater extent in this final generation, the 144,000, than in any other.

About the 144,000, Revelation says, "These are the ones who were not defiled with women, for they are virgins. These are the ones who follow the Lamb wherever He goes. These were redeemed from among men, being firstfruits to God and to the Lamb. And in their mouth was found no guile, for they are *without fault* before the throne of God" (Revelation 14:4, 5, emphasis supplied).

These people were "redeemed from among men." Since redemption comes only by the imputed righteousness of Christ, this group, therefore, have Christ as their legal substitute. But that fact doesn't diminish the reality of their sanctification. On the contrary, because they were redeemed they became holy. Holiness is part of redemption. The 144,000 demonstrate this holiness of character. They have pure doctrine (the "virgin" symbol), have "no guile in their mouth," and are "without fault before the throne of God."

These characteristics can't be said about everyone who is saved. They are not absolute prerequisites for salvation. The thief on the cross who accepted Christ had just been cursing Him earlier, so he hardly had "no guile in his mouth." As a thief, he wasn't "without fault." And, considering all the theological error of his time, it's not likely that his understanding of theology was pure either. Nevertheless, at that stage of his life, God took him as far as He could along the path of sanctification, and we have the words of Christ Himself that this man will be saved.

Anyone who is part of the final generation will have more character development than this thief ever accomplished. The thief didn't have the opportunity to experience what the 144,000 will experience. God doesn't expect as much from the thief in his short life as a believer as He expects from the living saints at the second coming. "Everyone to whom much is given, from him much will be required" (Luke 12:48). Someone whose character hasn't developed beyond that of the thief's, although he might be saved, wouldn't be among that final generation.

Perfection of the heart, along with holiness and sanctification, is relative. The 144,000 will come the farthest in their sanctification experience, even to the point that they can live without a mediator—but only because they have been "sealed" in the righteousness of Christ. They have made their decision to follow Christ no matter the cost. Their hearts are "perfect" toward God. They have proven their loyalty, even in the face of death. They would rather die than sin, and anyone who would rather die than sin—won't.

We're not talking about holy flesh, or sinlessness, in the sense of a changed nature. These people will still be fighting against the clamors of their fallen natures until glorification. And, if a billion years later, everyone in heaven will still be growing, then certainly the 144,000 won't have reached the apogee of holiness, love, and compassion at the second coming. Fully reflecting the image of Christ doesn't mean they equal it. Nevertheless, at this stage of their lives, under the unique circumstances they have been forced to go through during the time of trouble, they have remained faithful and obedient to God and to all His commandments. Their hearts are "perfect" toward God. "Here is the patience of the saints; here are those who keep the commandments of God and the faith of Jesus" (Revelation 14:12).

Why is it so hard to believe that the Creator of the universe can do this in the lives of people fully committed to Him? Jesus raised the dead, cast out demons, and perfectly healed the sick. Can't He work a miracle of sanctification so that He will have a people who—for a certain amount of time, at least, under unique circumstances—don't break the law?

With all the promises in Scripture about victory, overcoming, living a holy life, and being a "new creature" in Christ, why is the idea of God having a victorious people so hard to accept? Perhaps we are looking at ourselves and others around us, and not at God and His promises.

We're sinful, our hearts are corrupt, our natures perverted, our flesh carnal, but haven't we by faith been "crucified with Christ" (Galatians 2:20), so that "the body of sin might be done away with, that we should no longer be slaves of sin" (Romans 6:6)? "Those who are Christ's have crucified the flesh with its passions and desires" (Galatians 5:24). "Being confident of this very thing, that He who has begun a good work in you will complete it until the day of Jesus Christ" (Philippians 1:6). "By which have been given to us exceedingly great and precious promises, that through these you may be partakers of the divine nature, having escaped the corruption that is in the world through lust" (2 Peter 1:4).

Are these just nice theological statements, or can they be subjective experiences in the lives of all Christians, even now? Can't we envision the power of God working in His people until He has "a glorious church, not having spot or wrinkle or any such thing, but that it should be holy and without blemish" (Ephesians 5:27), even if we can't imagine ourselves being among it?

119

The Lord will have a law-abiding people who live after probation closes, after the temple is "filled with smoke from the glory of God and from his power" (Revelation 15:8), a people who have gained "the victory over the beast, over his image and over his mark and over the number of his name" (Revelation 15:2). It's a work that Christ does on their behalf to prepare them for the time when the "wrath of God" will be poured out in the seven last plagues, when evil will be "fully ripe" (Revelation 14:18), when the universe will witness the difference between those who are unjust and filthy and those who are righteous and holy just before the climax of the ages—the second coming of Jesus.

---

1. See also Numbers 1:53; 10:11; and Exodus 38:21.

2. "And when He [God] had made an end of speaking with him [Moses] on Mount Sinai, He gave Moses two tablets of the Testimony, tablets of stone, written with the finger of God" (Exodus 31:18). See also Exodus 34:29.

3. G. B. Caird, 200.

4. "While I was speaking in prayer, the man Gabriel, whom I had seen in the vision at the beginning . . ." (Daniel 9:21).

5. Davidson, "Sanctuary Typology."

6. "When Christ ceases His intercession in the sanctuary, the unmingled wrath threatened against those who worship the beast and his image and receive his mark (Revelation 14:9, 10), will be poured out. The plagues upon Egypt when God was about to deliver Israel were similar in character to those more terrible and extensive judgments which are to fall upon the world just before the final deliverance of God's people" (The Great Controversy, 627, 628).

"As Jesus moved out of the most holy place, I heard the tinkling of the bells upon His garment; and as He left, a cloud of darkness covered the inhabitants of the earth. There was then no mediator between guilty man and an offended God. While Jesus had been standing between God and guilty man, a restraint was upon the people; but when He stepped out from between man and the Father, the restraint was finally removed and Satan had entire control of the finally impenitent. It was impossible for the plagues to be poured out while Jesus officiated in the sanctuary; but as His work there is finished, and His intercession closes, there is nothing to stay the wrath of God, and it breaks with fury upon the shelterless head of the guilty sinner, who has slighted salvation and hated reproof. In that fearful time, after the close of Jesus' mediation, the saints were living in the sight of a holy God without an intercessor. Every case was decided, every jewel numbered" *(Early Writings,* 280).

7. Interestingly, the Bible calls someone else "perfect" as well. "Thou wast *perfect* in thy ways from the day that thou wast created, until iniquity was found in thee" (Ezekiel 28:15, KJV, emphasis supplied). Even Lucifer, at one point, at least, was considered "perfect." Obviously, whatever else "perfection" means, it means the ability to make wrong choices.

8. See William Richardson, "The Unfavorite Text," *Adventist Review* (14 October 1993), 8-10.

9. See *The Great Controversy,* 614.

"When Jesus ceases to plead for man, the cases of all are forever decided. This is the time of reckoning with His servants. To those who have neglected the preparation of purity and holiness, which fits them to be waiting ones to welcome their Lord, the sun sets in gloom and darkness, and rises not again. Probation closes; Christ's intercessions cease in heaven." *(Testimonies for the Church,* 2:191).

"I also saw that many do not realize what they must be in order to live in the sight of the Lord without a high priest in the sanctuary through the time of trouble. Those who receive the seal of the living God and are protected in the time of trouble must reflect the image of Jesus fully" *(Early Writings,* 71).

10. Beatrice S. Neall, "Sealed Saints and the Tribulation" in *Symposium on Revelation,* 276.

Chapter
Eleven
THE TABERNACLE OF GOD

T he final heavenly-sanctuary scene in Revelation, if not the climax of the earlier scenes, is—beyond question— their consummation. All the previous sanctuary scenes in Revelation have led to, and prepared the way for, this final one.

After the close of probation, depicted in Revelation, chapter 15, John describes the havoc that follows—the plagues, the war against "Him who sat on the horse" (Revelation 19:21), Satan's final assault, and the millennial eradication of the wicked— events that are associated with the end of the world. With everything from people gnawing their tongues in pain, to birds nibbling on human flesh, to the wicked being consumed with fire, it's not a pretty, or painless, conclusion.

Fortunately, the story doesn't end with the last verse of Revelation 20: "And anyone not found written in the Book of Life was cast into the lake of fire" (verse 15). Two more chapters follow, and the first begins: "And I saw a new heaven and a new earth, for the first heaven and the first earth had passed away. Also there was no more sea. Then I, John, saw the holy city, New Jerusalem, coming down out of heaven from God, prepared as a bride adorned for her husband" (Revelation 21:1, 2).

These verses show what was also shown by Daniel's vision (in chapter 2) of a stone that struck and crushed the great multimetal image of the world kingdoms. Both visions show that salvation climaxes, not with a modification of the existing world order, but with a radical remaking of reality.

"Behold, I make all things new" (Revelation 21:5).

"For behold, I create new heavens and a new earth: and the former shall not be remembered or come to mind" (Isaiah 65:17).

"Nevertheless we, according to His promise, look for new heavens and a new earth in which righteousness dwells" (2 Peter 3:13).

It's in this context—of a new heaven, a new earth, and a new Jerusalem—that the next sanctuary scene appears.[1] "I heard a loud voice from heaven saying, 'Behold the *tabernacle* of God is with men, and He will dwell with them, and they shall be His people, and God Himself will be with them and be their God' " (Revelation 21:3, emphasis supplied).

The tabernacle, of course, is another name for the sanctuary. In this case, however, it's not the wilderness sanctuary or the first or second temple or even the heavenly edifice, because in verse 22 John is clear that no temple exists in the New Jerusalem: "I saw no temple in it, for the Lord God Almighty and the Lamb are its temple."

What has happened to the heavenly sanctuary, so clearly depicted in both Testaments?

Why was there a sanctuary in heaven at all? Wasn't it part of God's plan to eradicate sin? At this stage, after the destruction of Satan and the unredeemed and the appearance of the new heaven and earth, there's no temple because there's no longer any need for it! Sin and unredeemed sinners are no more. Salvation has been completed. Instead of having to draw near a building or enter the heavenly sanctuary by faith, the redeemed can now enjoy the presence of God Himself. Now, John says, "the tabernacle of God is with men, and He will dwell with them" (verse 3).

The word *tabernacle* comes from the same Greek root that appears in John 1:14 in reference to Christ's incarnation: "The Word became flesh and *dwelt* among us" (emphasis supplied). This verb means also "to pitch a tent." The noun form used in Revelation 21:3 is also the same Greek word used in the Septuagint for the Hebrew word *shekinah,* designating God's glory, which appeared in the Most Holy Place of the sanctuary.

"The voice from heaven," writes Mounce, "declares that the

tabernacle of God is with men and that He shall dwell with them. The Greek word for tabernacle (*skene*) is closely related to the Hebrew *shekinah*, which was used to denote the presence and glory of God. In the wilderness wanderings the tabernacle or tent was a symbol of the abiding presence of God in the midst of His people. In the Fourth Gospel, John writes that the Word became flesh and tabernacled (*eskenosen*) among men so that they beheld his glory, glory as the only Son from the Father (Jn 1:14). When the seer writes that the tabernacle of God is with men, he is saying that God in his glorious presence has come to dwell with man. The metaphor does not suggest a temporary dwelling. From this point on, God remains with his people throughout eternity."[2]

Exactly what this manifestation of God's presence will be, Revelation doesn't say. Today, we recognize His presence through His Spirit, which we grasp by faith, not by sight. But Scripture teaches that the time will come when, instead, we "shall see His face" (Revelation 22:4), when "we shall see Him as He is" (1 John 3:2), when we shall know just as also we are known (see 1 Corinthians 13:12).

"This is a reality," writes Ladd, "that we cannot visualize; but direct unmarred fellowship between God and His people is the goal of all redemption."[3]

Indeed, what is the ultimate purpose of the Christian faith? Is it just to live holy lives here on earth, then finally pop a pipe, break a line, and sputter out with no hope of something beyond what we experience in this life? Is Christianity simply to love the Lord with all our heart, all our soul, all our mind, and our neighbor as ourselves—and then to wind up ultimately where our neighbors do as well, disintegrating into the ground? Did Christ live, suffer, and die just to teach us the love of God and how to live morally?

Actually, one doesn't even need Christianity to live a moral life. Many other religions, even philosophies, espouse morality and have produced "moral" people. For example, Immanuel Kant in his *Foundations for a Metaphysics of Morality*, posited with his "categorical imperative" a moral system higher than what most Christians would find even in the Bible. However important it may be to visit widows and orphans in their affliction, there must be more to Christianity than ethical living. If all Christ did was to teach us to live a better way, then the difference between Him and Buddha, Mohammed, and Gandhi is minimal.

Yet neither Buddha, Mohammed, nor Gandhi could do what Jesus has done and will do, because none of them was who Jesus was. Because of who He was—One "equal with God" (Philippians 2:6)—Jesus alone could pay the penalty of sin, not just so we could be accounted holy but so the rupture between humans and God could be healed and redeemed humanity could once again enjoy an unbroken fellowship with the Creator.

Unbroken fellowship forever with Christ is the ultimate purpose of salvation,[4] and the verse promising that the "tabernacle of God" will be with men (Revelation 21:3) is referring to this eternal, unbroken fellowship. Without it, Christianity offers nothing of perpetual value.

The promise says, too, that not only will God dwell with the redeemed, but that "they shall be His people, and God Himself will be with them and be their God." Here, again, is the promise of a special relationship the redeemed will enjoy with the Lord. This verse is a modification of the covenant vow the Lord had made with national Israel more than 2,500 years ago: "I will set My tabernacle among you, and My soul shall not abhor you. I will walk among you and be your God, and you shall be My people" (Leviticus 26:11, 12). This pledge was repeated by the prophets centuries later: "You shall be My people, and I will be your God" (Jeremiah 30:22). "You shall dwell in the land that I gave to your fathers; you shall be My people, and I will be your God" (Ezekiel 36:28). "I will deliver them from all their dwelling places in which they have sinned, and will cleanse them. Then they shall be My people, and I will be their God" (Ezekiel 37:23).[5]

No doubt, the fellowship believers have had with God on earth, when even Moses could see only a glimpse of Him ("You cannot see My face; for no man shall see Me, and live" [Exodus 33:20]), is nothing compared to John's description of what we will experience in the new earth, when we, indeed, "shall see His face"

(Revelation 22:4).

Why? Because sin—the intruder that originated the rupture between God and humanity[6]—has been eradicated! The relationship is restored. The central purpose of the plan of salvation is to deal with the problem of sin—because sin caused the break between humans and God, and that break caused humans to die. The gift of eternal life is simply the restoration of what was originally ours. Jesus came, lived, died, was resurrected, ministers in the heavenly sanctuary, and will come again—all as part of the divine plan to eradicate sin and its greatest consequence: death.

The book of Revelation, especially the heavenly-sanctuary scenes, is a behind-the-scenes look at God's activity in dealing with sin—not just as the Lamb when He was upon earth, not just as the Lion at His second coming, but in His role as High Priest in between. Nowhere else does the New Testament so graphically depict the heavenly activity on behalf of sinners or give such a detailed look at what happens in the heavenly sanctuary. Hebrews teaches that Christ ministers there as our High Priest; Revelation gives us an inside look at that ministry.

The purpose of the sanctuary service, beginning with the cross, was to deal with sin; the purpose of the book of Revelation, with the sanctuary as its background, is to show the Lord dealing with sin—via the sanctuary—and the wonderful results when He's finished. Not only will God tabernacle with the redeemed in the new earth, but He "will wipe away every tear from their eyes; there shall be no more death, nor sorrow, nor crying; and there shall be no more pain, for the former things have passed away" (Revelation 21:4).

The basic structure of the sanctuary scenes in Revelation elaborates on this point. The Apocalypse, as we saw in chapter 2 of this book, begins with the death of Christ as well as with His presence among His people on the earth. Besides the references to the cross, there is the vision of Christ among the candlesticks, which are "the seven churches" (Revelation 1:20). The emphasis is earthly. Then, for the next four scenes, the venue shifts to heaven: the first apartment of the heavenly sanctuary (see Revelation 4–5; 8:2-6), and then the second apartment (see

Revelation 11:19; 15:5-8). In the final sanctuary scene (Revelation 21), the focus returns to earth, where it remains forever. Strand writes:

> In the first introductory scene, John sees the Christ who had come as God incarnate in His first advent—who was killed and then resurrected, and who ascended to heaven after 40 days. Now this same Divine Person appears to John as the one who was dead but lives forever (Revelation 1:17-18) and is present, walking among His churches/ lampstands. This first victorious-introduction scene thus evidences the continual and close presence of this very Jesus with His church on earth. . . . The counterpart of this divine presence in the "here-and-now" is the fullness of the experience of the divine presence contingent upon Jesus's second advent to bring rewards to all persons according to their deeds (Rev. 22:12). In the final stages of those rewards—that is the "new heaven"/"new earth"/New Jerusalem experience—God and the Lamb again "tabernacle" with their people, but now this tabernacling is an immediate and direct presence.[7]

What this movement from earth to heaven and back to earth proves is that salvation centers on Christ and follows Him wherever He goes. He began His work of salvation on earth, went to the sanctuary in heaven to administer it to us (Revelation's central theme), and once done He will return to earth to enjoy the "travail of His soul" (Isaiah 53:11) as He tabernacles with His people.

In the book of Revelation, then, we follow Christ on His journey as the Lamb, the Lion, and His role in between. And, through faith in His blood, those who "follow the Lamb wherever He goes" (Revelation 14:4) will end that journey in the new heaven and the new earth with Him.

> And there shall be no more curse, but the throne of God and of the Lamb shall be in it, and His servants shall serve Him. They shall see His face, and His name shall be on

their foreheads. And there shall be no night there: They need no lamp nor light of the sun, for the Lord God gives them light. And they shall reign forever and ever (Revelation 22:3-5).

---

1. Strand has Revelation 19:1-10 as the next sanctuary scene. He bases this identification mostly on the fact that some of the imagery and setting parallel the first heavenly sanctuary scene in chapters 4 and 5—a strong point. As do the other scenes, it also introduces something that happens on earth—the second coming of Jesus (see Revelation 19:11-21), obviously an event of major importance. Yet in Revelation 19:1-10, there are no explicit images from the sanctuary, which leaves this passage suspect as a sanctuary scene. For that reason, I footnote it rather than place it in the general text, although it could be argued that it is nevertheless a heavenly-sanctuary scene. Perhaps, the reason that sanctuary imagery isn't explicit in this passage is that the heavenly sanctuary has dropped from view because Christ's work in it is done.

2. Mounce, 371, 372.

3. Ladd, 277.

4. This doesn't deal with the questions regarding the law of God, His character, and the issues behind the great controversy. "But the plan of redemption had yet a broader and deeper purpose than the salvation of man. It was not for this alone that Christ came to the earth; it was not merely that the inhabitants of this little world might regard the law of God as it should be regarded; but it was to vindicate the character of God before the universe. . . . The act of Christ in dying for the salvation of man would not only make heaven accessible to men, but before all the universe it would justify God and His Son in their dealing with the rebellion of Satan. It would establish the perpetuity of the law of God and would reveal the nature and results of sin" *(Patriarchs and Prophets*, 68, 69).

5. See also Jeremiah 7:23; 11:4.

6. "By sin man was shut out from God. Except for the plan of redemption, eternal separation from God, the darkness of unending night, would have been his. Through the Saviour's sacrifice, communion with God is again made possible. We may not in person approach into His presence; in our sin we may not look upon His face; but we can commune with Him in Jesus, the Saviour" *(Education,* 28).

7. Strand, "Victorious-Introduction Scenes," 70.